CHASING THE AMISH DREAM

PL△INSPOKEN
Real-life stories of Amish and Mennonites

"Loren Beachy is such a charmer! Reading through these delightful stories of life as an Amish bachelor, I felt like I was with Loren at an old-fashioned box social, a farm auction, and all the places and spaces he occupies in his plain community. Jump in the buggy with Loren Beachy and you'll take to this book like a rabbit to a carrot patch."
—*Lorilee Craker, author of* Money Secrets of the Amish

"Beachy's witty and charming stories capture the joy and delight of Amish life."
—*Donald B. Kraybill, author of* The Riddle of Amish Culture

"I can assure you that you will not only devour this refreshing and hilarious read. You will gain a newfound understanding of the Amish as a people. You will realize that we, too, are individuals created in flesh and blood."
—*Michael Lambright, Amish teacher*

"From the classroom and the ball field to canoe trips with friends, cross-country jaunts, and horse auctions, these engaging vignettes open a window into life in Loren Beachy's northern Indiana Amish community. A fun and informative read!"
—*Karen Johnson-Weiner, coauthor of* The Amish

CHASING THE AMISH DREAM

MY LIFE AS A YOUNG AMISH BACHELOR

LOREN BEACHY

Herald Press

Harrisonburg, Virginia
Kitchener, Ontario

Library of Congress Cataloging-in-Publication Data
Beachy, Loren, 1987- author.
  Chasing the Amish dream : my life as a young Amish bachelor / Loren Beachy.
     pages cm
  Includes bibliographical references.
  ISBN 978-0-8361-9907-9 (pbk. : alk. paper) 1. Beachy, Loren, 1987-
2. Amish—Indiana—Goshen—Biography. I. Title.
  BX8143.B38A3 2014
  289.7092--dc23
  [B]
                                    2014028460

CHASING THE AMISH DREAM
Copyright © 2014 by Herald Press, Harrisonburg, Virginia 22802
    Released simultaneously in Canada by Herald Press, Kitchener, Ontario
    N2G 3R1. All rights reserved.
Library of Congress Control Number: 2014028460
International Standard Book Number: 978-0-8361-9907-9
Printed in the United States of America
Cover and interior design by Merrill Miller
Cover composite image created from photographs by Doyle Yoder, Susan
    Miller, and Wayne Gehman

Unless otherwise noted, Scripture text is quoted from the *King James Version*.

To order or request information, please call 1-800-245-7894 in the United
States or 1-800-631-6535 in Canada. Or visit www.heraldpress.com.

18 17 16 15 14   10 9 8 7 6 5 4 3 2 1

Chapters that first appeared as The Plain Side columns in the *Goshen News* and that are adapted or reprinted with permission from the *Goshen News* include the following: **Part I** "Bouncy Belinda": April 28, 2012; "The Defeat of Chipper Chester": October 17, 2009; "Box Social": October 27, 2012; "A Sister's Logic": November 7, 2009; "A Borrowed Bike and a Wheeled Chair": December 3, 2011; "Soggy Cycling": June 13, 2009; "A Bass Pro": June 14, 2014; "The Gifted Lloyd Yoder": December 18, 2010; "Lloyd Yoder Reprise": December 31, 2010; "The Kansas Andy Boys' Good Deed": November 24, 2012. **Part II** "If You Get Out of Your Buggy, Get Ready to Run": May 4, 2013; "Spelling Bee Jitters": March 22, 2014; "Wisecrack Wanda": February 7, 2009; "That Gilligan Can Run": December 14, 2010; "Windy Willy's Hot Axe": December 19, 2009; "Auctions and Pranks": February 18, 2012; "The Whiteboard Wars": October 22, 2011; "The Pen Is Mightier than the Breakfast Burrito": January 16, 2010; "The Grand Canyon in Winter": January 30 and February 13, 2010; "The Children of Israel Enter Rural Topeka": March 8, 2014. **Part III** "School Visitation": April 6, 2013; "Sign Your Notes, Smarty!": January 19, 2013; "Wisecrack Wanda's Slump": April 9, 2011; "Mudville Madness": February 4, 2012; "The Shellacking": July 21, 2012; "Murder Mountain": August 4, 2012; "My Friend, the Legend": August 18, 2012; "The Brick Landed in Pennsylvania": September 15, 2012; "God's Quilt": May 31, 2014. **Part IV** "The Best West Quest": July 27, August 10, and August 24, 2013; "Golden Gate Bridge": September 7 and 13, 2013; "How Do You Play Basketball?": October 5 and 19, 2013; "Conquering Upper Yosemite Falls": November 2 and 16, 2013; "Final Legs of the Best West Quest": December 14 and 28, 2013, and January 11, 2014; "How the Catfish Cleans His Teeth": May 29, 2010; "Hay Bales": July 6, 2013; "The Kansas Andy Boys Strike Again": December 8, 2012; "Canoe Chivalry": July 13, 2013; "Bucket List": February 23, 2013.

*To my dad, who taught me to think
logically, historically, and spiritually.*

*And to my mom, who, more than anyone,
instilled in me a love of all things literary.*

*And most of all to God, from whom all
blessings flow.*

CONTENTS

PART III: SPRING

PART IV: SUMMER

INTRODUCTION TO

PL◬INSPOKEN

Real-life stories of Amish and Mennonites

AMISH NOVELS, Amish tourist sites, and Amish-themed TV shows offer second- or third-hand accounts of Amish and Mennonite life. Some of these messages are sensitive and accurate. Some are not. Many are flat-out wrong.

Now readers can listen directly to the voices of the Amish themselves through Plainspoken: Real-Life Stories of Amish and Mennonites. In the books in this series, readers get to hear Amish and Mennonite writers talk about the texture of their daily lives: how they spend their time, what they value, what makes them laugh, and how they summon strength from their Christian faith and community.

The Amish are publishing their writing more than ever before. In periodicals like *Die Botschaft* and *The Budget*, Amish writers across Canada and the United States connect with each other. Amish printing presses and publishing houses bring books by Amish authors to Amish readers. But such magazines and books are read mostly by other Amish and Mennonites and rarely by the larger reading public.

Until now. Now readers can learn what authentic Amish life looks and feels like—from the inside out. The Amish and Mennonites have stories to tell. Through Plainspoken, readers get the chance to hear them.

AUTHOR'S NOTE

IN A FEW OF THE PERSONALITY PROFILES, such as Chipper Chester, Wisecrack Wanda, and Bouncy Belinda, I may have combined two personalities, added minor details or happenings, or changed names. And as I imagine all authors do, I sometimes filled in small details as I thought they might have been or could have been. The year you are about to enjoy with me is also a composite, as these events did not all happen in the same calendar year.

With that said, you are reading a collection of true stories.

—*Loren Beachy*

A DAY IN THE LIFE OF THE AUTHOR

The best way to make your dreams come true
is to wake up.
—J. M. Power

TUESDAY, AUGUST 25

3:50 a.m. I reset the alarm clock for 4:20. This would give me another half hour or so of precious sleep. Before then, though, I am awakened by the crunch of tires on gravel. Brother Johnny's driver has carted him off to Keystone, the RV factory where he works.

Well, that's better yet. Now that he's out of the way, I can enjoy a morning shower in peace. I rather like this time of day to take a shower. There is no one bellowing at me to hurry up, demanding to know how long I'll be, or messing with my water supply by turning it on elsewhere in the house. With six siblings on the second floor of the house, the bathroom is a precious commodity indeed.

4:45 a.m. The quiet time afterward is right up there with the morning shower on the list of simple pleasures. After packing my lunch, I park myself at the kitchen table with the Word of God and a hot drink. This is quite a pleasant way to start the day.

The fall sometimes seems to be one long rush hour for me. Some days hold an auction, some hold a classroom of lovable students, and many days include both. Today is one of the latter. Rush or no rush, I get to chase my dream of being both a teacher and an auctioneer. I am a blessed man. Thank you, Lord.

5:30 a.m. After breakfast I shuffle a few papers in my office across the driveway and send a fax from the phone shack behind it. Then it's off to school on my racer. Race bike, that is. Just out of the shop, it shifts smoothly and operates efficiently as I pedal the six-plus miles to my school. This predawn ride through the cool air often does much to clear my brain of any lingering cobwebs. I arrive at school charged and ready.

I am perhaps a bit earlier than usual, and neither of my co-teachers, Delmar and Margaret, has arrived yet. This is the time to scan the lessons for today and put the schedule on our whiteboard.

6:45 a.m. One group of children often arrives half an hour early. Fortunately, they are quite capable of helping out if need be. Today we put them to work marking the school's name in a new batch of library books. A few of them are busy with this as the rest of the scholars arrive.

7:25 a.m. Delmar rings the bell. Yep, we start early. He leads us in devotions, including a Bible story, the Lord's Prayer, and singing.

Classes commence. Second grade has a timed drill on addition this morning, and these five excited youngsters all ace it, finishing well under the required minute. Their delight is contagious as I place a star on their charts.

Third grade has a lesson on story problems, which we discuss. Students in fourth, seventh, and eighth grades are often able to figure out their lessons for themselves with little explanation from me.

9:00 a.m. Too soon, it is recess time. We enjoy a spirited game of "darebase," a fast-paced contest in which contestants attempt to catch opponents off their base and capture them for their own team. Thus, we are better prepared to tackle English and some reading between now and lunchtime.

10:30 a.m. At lunchtime I run to the phone and make a few calls while I eat. We are facing an advertising deadline and are trying to get an auction flyer finalized.

One of the school day's highlights is the ball game after we eat. This is my week to join our twelve first and second graders on the small diamond. What they lack in power and know-how is often amply compensated for with enthusiasm. A solid hit is deemed worthy of comment, and catching a pop fly is cause for delight.

Lunch break is followed by a story, where I read aloud a portion of *Cheaper by the Dozen* to the third through eighth graders. Margaret reads to our first and second graders in an adjoining room.

11:45 a.m. The rest of the school day moves by quickly. A group of students cleans the schoolhouse during the last recess at 12:45, and we dismiss everyone at the usual 1:50. Yep, we finish early.

2:30 p.m. After hurrying through some grading, I hustle homeward so I can peek at and approve the flyer proof, faxed by LaGwana Printing, before I leave for the auction tonight. I change clothes, tell Mom where I'm going, and cycle the three miles to the auction house.

4:10 p.m. The sale tonight is at Middlebury Auction Center. We are selling the Mallette estate, which has been hauled down here from Emma. Ferman Yoder, the owner of the auction center, has coordinated the hauling and much of the help for the auction.

A healthy crowd is already milling through the huge selection of items when I arrive shortly after four o'clock. I dash into Ferman's phone shack first and call Scott Signs. We need to change the time on some panels they are making for us.

5:00 p.m. We make final preparations in the auction house and enjoy chatting with a few of the attendees before making our announcements and starting at five o'clock. A healthy crowd is here, as well as a huge amount of merchandise, so we kick off promptly with two rings. John Troyer, a fellow auctioneer and friend, sells in one ring, and I sell the items along the wall opposite him, trying to keep the auction snappy.

We do pause long enough, though, to enjoy a chuckle with Virgil Ropp and his wife, who unknowingly begin to bid against each other on an item. Of course, we let them off the hook and start over.

After an hour or so, John is done with his row and replaces me. We go outside to sell some items. When that's finished, my crew and I make for the far end of the auction house to sell bigger items such as furniture.

Ryan Lambright, a fine young auctioneer, has taken my friend John's place. John replaces me, and after a break, I replace Ryan again on the front auction block. The Mallette family's appliances sell fairly well to an eager crowd. We wind down with smaller items.

9:30 p.m. After finishing the auction and thanking the attendees, I chat with Ferman, a black-bearded, solidly built thirty-something who has been a solid business associate for several years. Then I collect my pay and hop back onto my trusty cycle for the homeward jaunt.

This quiet bike ride home through the dark is a good time to reflect on the day. Selling quality items to a happy crowd willing to pay a fair price is what makes this job exciting and satisfying. I suppose the pleasurable part is a bit like teaching in that great satisfaction comes from teaching worthwhile knowledge to eager minds.

Thank you, Lord. I get to live the dream. I get to do both.

PART I

Autumn

1

LATE FOR CHURCH

PUFFING AND STEAMING, I turn my trusty maroon bicycle into the driveway. The biggest concern running (and running and running) through my mind for this thirty-minute bike trip? I might be late for church.

Church services are at Menno and Mary Lehman's home today. This is not my home district, but Menno's children are my students. It is customary for us to attend church services held at the home of our acquaintances or relatives. It is not customary to arrive late. In fact, it is downright embarrassing.

I calculate that it must be close to nine o'clock as I whip into the driveway of the *dawdy* house adjacent to Menno's place. Anonymity would be nice.

Clambering off the bicycle, I quickly remove my rainsuit and rubber boots. I listen carefully for the sound of singing. Nothing. I may be in time.

I jam my black hat onto my head and leave the stocking cap I wore for the ride on my bicycle. I hustle around the *dawdy* house toward Menno's place, where services are to be held.

The sound of singing reaches my ears. Cue sinking feeling. Everyone, including some of my students, will see me walk in late.

If I stay, that is. I could still turn around, hop on my bike, and go back home, maybe without anyone even realizing I had been there.

What would Jesus do, right?

Hmmm, Jesus would probably be on time to start with. But now that I'm faced with the choice of walking in late or scampering back home, what now?

I actually turn around and retreat a few steps. In the pressure of the moment, I at least want to hide behind the house while I ponder the choice.

It is not to be. The door to the house opens just I pass it. Menno's mother, Lizzie, had come back across the yard to her *dawdy* house, which was built for her and her husband when their children took over the farmette. She was apparently retrieving something and is now returning to church. I am caught.

"Just go on in," Lizzie urges kindly. She has taken the situation in at a glance. "I'll make room for you."

Well, it's too late to go home anonymously now anyway. I steel myself and turn back toward church.

"You weren't just going to leave, were you?" Lizzie is almost indignant.

I sure was thinking about it.

• • •

I place my hat in the usual spot—in the empty bench wagon outside the door of the church building. Since most of the benches are inside the building, the bench wagon is an ideal spot for storing hats out of the weather during the three-hour services.

Nervously, I comb my hair with my fingers. All eyes will be upon me in a few moments, and not for any praiseworthy reason.

Mentally gritting my teeth, I open the door and step inside. Lizzie has arranged for a spot on a bench just inside the door. I appreciate this. The singing has continued unabated, but I know some of my keen-minded friends in the room are calculating the best way to poke fun at my tardiness later.

I sit down and accept the songbook handed to me by a grinning neighbor. I place my fogged glasses on my knee—my physical exertions and the relative heat of the room are steaming them up—and pay close attention to my songbook for a while.

Church is usually a rejuvenating experience, as a fellowship of believers is intended to be, I suppose. I expect today will be enjoyable too, after we get past the less than ideal beginning.

This "family room" was recently added on to Menno's house. It has a concrete floor, and Mary likely does her laundry here. When it is Menno's family's turn to host church services, this room has enough space to seat a few hundred people on wooden benches brought in from the bench wagon. Quilts hanging on the walls and primitive tools on shelves add to the homey feel and remind us of times gone by.

The benches are set up in three sections around a T-shaped aisle. We men and boys are seated on either side of the stem of the T facing each other. The preacher will stand at the base of the stem and face the ladies, who are sitting in the biggest section across the top of the T.

For now, though, the preachers have filed out of the church room as usual to hold a short council and pray. We sing while they're gone.

The first song ends and there is a pause of perhaps a minute allowing us to meditate or pray. "*Siebenhundert siebenzig*" rings across the church room. The page number of the next song is 770. This second song is called the *Lob Lied* ("Praise Song") and is the only melody we sing every Sunday. It includes praise for our God, prayer for the preachers and listeners, and a plea for God's presence.

After giving out the page number, the song leader, Verlin Miller, asks a few men to lead it. As is the custom, one man agrees to lead the first two verses and another the final two.

I am slightly on edge while Verlin is asking fellows to lead this song. Usually the married men lead the songs, but occasionally single boys who are church members, like myself, are asked to lead.

Not today. Two men agree to lead and the song begins with the familiar "*O Gott Vater . . . .*" As our church has done for hundreds of years, we sing in a slow fashion. Tradition says our persecuted Anabaptist forebears, forbidden to sing while in prison, developed slow tunes to disguise their songs from their captors. This slow style is a constant reminder of what our forefathers endured. It takes about twenty minutes to sing the four verses of the *Lob Lied*.

After we've sung the *Lob Lied*, we start another song when the preachers return. We cut this short after one verse.

The standard number of ministers in a church district is four, including one bishop, two preachers, and a deacon. This is supplemented today, as it often is, by visiting ministers from across the community.

Vernon Miller, a blocky man with a full black beard, stands up to deliver a message first. He has the *Anfang* (beginning) today.

After speaking for fifteen to twenty minutes about the importance of community as well as the Christmas story, Vernon leads us in prayer and sits down.

Everyone stands. It is time to read one of today's Scriptures—Orv Mullet's task this time.

Orv, a visiting deacon, has been doing this for a while. Our Scriptures today are the Christmas story in Luke. Orv reads it with expression and fervor, in German, as usual. I am glad some of my students are here. Orv is modeling excellent reading technique.

When Orv finishes Luke 1, we all take our seats again, and Marlin Hochstetler stands to deliver the main part of the sermon.

Marlin was ordained less than a year ago and, with our church's lack of formal training for preachers, could be excused for struggling. Prayer is powerful, though, and despite being obviously nervous, Marlin does a fine job. He spices his sermon with stories and finishes by reading Luke 2, the other chapter of today's Scripture.

As usual, at the end of Marlin's "main part" sermon, he asks the home bishop, Menno, for testimony on the accuracy of content. Marlin also requests that Menno ask a few others for testimony. This is the "proofreading" process, if you will, meant to ensure that we hear a sound sermon and follow biblical teaching that "in the mouth of two or three witnesses shall every word be established" (2 Corinthians 13:1).

After the testimony by four of the other preachers, Marlin leads us in prayer. Bishop Menno then has a few announcements. These messages often include upcoming charity auctions, sewings, or church projects as well as announcing where church will be held next time, Lord willing. Today the announcements consist mostly of medical expenses of the community that our church members' pooled money pays for, as well as an explanation of our new community system for paying each other's medical costs in response to the Affordable Care Act.

When Menno finishes, Verlin announces the page number of the last song and chooses someone to lead it. The final notes of the song fade away, marking the end of services. The young boys are quick to get off their benches and head outside to romp in the fresh air until lunch is ready.

The men who live in this church district quickly gather together the songbooks and assemble tables for lunch. The rest of us huddle in small groups and begin to chat while the ladies set the tables for lunch.

Now I begin to hear it.

"Your alarm clock getting dusty?"

"Did you have a fresh cow?"

"We usually start at nine o'clock."

You get the picture. Since this is no more than I would dish out if the situation were reversed, I'd better grin and bear it.

After the required ribbing, we spend time catching up with old acquaintances and discussing new happenings. Some feel this social time before, during, and after our Sunday lunch is one of the essential ties that binds together our community.

Once we are seated at the tables, we bow our heads for a few moments in silent prayer. Today we enjoy the usual bread, peanut butter, jelly, pickles, pickled beets, ham, and cheese. In a nod to Christmas coming in a few days, we are treated to some utterly delicious pie for dessert instead of the standard cookies.

Lunch over and a few goodbyes said, I stroll back to my bicycle. Many of the families will stay to socialize for another hour or so. I, however, have a vision of a Sunday afternoon nap dancing in my head.

2

BOUNCY BELINDA

BELINDA BOUNCES THROUGH the classroom door with a cheery "Good morning, Teacher!" After depositing her lunch box at her hook, she swiftly patters over to the cluster of students gathered at one end of the classroom. She is drawn by the curiosity that pervades all of humankind, especially seven-year-olds. She needs to see what all the others are checking out.

After investigating, the lass's eye is caught by the flower she planted that is sitting in a cup on the windowsill. Minutely, she examines the tiny flowerpot for signs of growth. Finding nothing, the charming damsel's attention finally falls on the stack of books waiting on her desk.

"Oh, yes! I still need to check my books," she exclaims and smiles half-sheepishly in my direction, aware that I have been watching her with amused toleration on my face. It would be nice to see the girl tend to business a bit more, but she does get things done—and in inimitable fashion.

Now the enthusiastic seven-year-old lass is doing her job for the morning, looking over her lessons from the day before.

"Yay! A 100 percent!" she cries. And a bit later, "Oh, bummer, I just missed one that time."

Bragging? Not a bit. These celebrations spring from sheer unbridled exuberance and an innocent spirit.

Bouncy Belinda has arrived here at Sunrise Valley School.

• • •

The bell rings. The school day here at Sunrise Valley commences with devotions. All three classes congregate in the largest classroom. To make room, students sit together.

Bouncy Belinda finds a tall thirteen-year-old girl to sit with and smiles disarmingly. A grin splits the older girl's face as she scoots over to make room. Some would call Belinda "adorable"; some, "huggable." Whatever she is, she is easy to like.

After participating in devotions and singing with gusto, Belinda returns to her own seat for the start of classes. It's school time.

I call Belinda's class. After first grade is gathered around the table, I present them with a page of pictures they will need to name in writing.

One picture baffles first grade. Bouncy Belinda, though, has a feeling she has seen it before. This picture looks like something she saw hanging above the busy intersection in town.

"It's a . . . a . . . a . . . *light stopper!*" she declares. I feel a sudden need to cough into my sleeve; then I redirect the conversation.

The fun and games are not over yet. After awhile it's time for math class, and today first grade is introduced to the quarter coin.

I hand each young scholar a quarter, and after giving them just a moment to examine it, I open discussion with a question: "Does anyone know who the man is on the front of the quarter?" This could be interesting.

Belinda's classmate guesses it is Abraham Lincoln. I point out that this is a good guess, but while Honest Abe is on the penny, that is not him on the quarter.

A few more guesses and first grade's supply of possibilities is almost exhausted. Bouncy Belinda, though, has one more shot. Fear of being wrong is not a big obstacle for Belinda.

I turn to Belinda, who is jabbing her hand into the air and almost panting in fear that she will not be called on. "Yes, Belinda, who do you think that man is?"

Belinda's hand finally comes down, and she says with unfeigned eagerness, "Is it John the Baptist?"

I am seized by another coughing fit.

• • •

Finally, the last bell of the school day sounds and Bouncy Belinda, after being dismissed, bounces around the schoolroom doing first this, now that, in preparation to go home. Belinda's brothers are already outside, hitching the pony.

Suddenly, Belinda realizes the schoolhouse is almost empty and she must hustle to avoid making her brothers wait for her. Grabbing her pink lunch box, she barrels out the door. Belinda, all four feet of her, sprints down the hill with covering and bonnet strings streaming in the wind. She makes it into the cart seat just as her older brother clucks to the pony. They're off.

I had been helping the boys hitch their steed and as I watch them go, Bouncy Belinda makes a point of turning around in her seat, raising her arm in a huge wave, and calling, "See ya, Loren."

A smile splits my face. "See ya, Belinda."

3

THE DEFEAT OF CHIPPER CHESTER

CHIPPER CHESTER is doing a slow dance around the classroom before the morning bell. With a gently fluttering pack of papers waving in his hand, an impromptu song issues from Chester's mouth. The song goes something like this:

Oh, yes I got a hundred
Oh, yes I got a hundred
Oh, yes I got a hundred, again.

The happy melody refers to the fact that Chester just discovered he aced his vocabulary quiz. He scored a perfect 100 percent.

Song now over, Chester ceases dancing and flashes a jolly grin at his classmates, who are rolling their eyes at Chester's goofiness, yet laughing in spite of themselves.

Celebration over, Chester moves to put his pack of quizzes back on the rack. There is a bounce to his step and a cheery whistle coming from his mouth. Chipper Chester's celebration springs not from conceit. Uh-uh. Nope. Rather, it is Chester's enthusiastic spirit bubbling up and over. Perhaps that is why his classmates accept and even enjoy the quick celebration instead of resenting the whole thing.

Chester's ability to forget himself and let his personality show makes for some light moments during the school day.

• • •

One blustery fall day during recess at Sunrise Valley, a hot ball game is brewing, which seems to take much of the chill out of the air. Chipper Chester is in his element and having a blast.

When it is Chester's turn to bat, the outfielders stand back. They are wary of Chester's solid drives deep into the outfield.

Chester notices the significant gap between the infielders and the outfielders as he steps up to the plate. A sparkle dances in Chester's eyes as he waits for the first pitch.

When the pitch arrives, Chester swings his trusty bat almost in a chopping manner, in a downward motion. He connects solidly and whacks the ball quickly through the infield, but as planned, it lands far short of the distant outfielders.

Chipper Chester is out of the box like a shot, rounds first, and is halfway to second base before an outfielder even picks up the ball. Chester cruises into second base with a standing two-bagger.

"What were you doing all the way out there? Hunting rabbits?" Chester chirps cheerfully to the outfielders as he catches his breath on second base.

Wisecrack Wanda is playing left field. "You just wait 'til it's my turn to bat!" she flares. "I'm going to burn you so bad, you'll *wish* you were hunting rabbits."

Chester is unruffled and merely laughs off Wanda's threat. The next time Chester bats, the outfielders move in a step or two but still leave too much room and Chipper Chester chops in another double in front of the outfielders. The game is an offensive battle, and Chester's double temporarily gives his team the lead.

Wisecrack Wanda's next at-bat comes in the top of the seventh inning. She hustles out an infield grounder to tie the game. The knowledge that the game is now tied helps Wanda turn a deaf ear to Chester's chirping from the outfield. This chatter is aimed at reminding Wanda of the dire promise she just made to burn him.

The game remains tied in the bottom of the seventh inning when Chipper Chester comes up to bat. His team has a runner on third base and two outs.

The pitcher pauses for a moment while the outfielders have a conference. They agree on one thing. Measures must be taken to prevent Chester from chopping in another double in front of them. Such a hit would win the game.

When the outfielders scatter again, Rifle-Arm Richard only goes out about halfway as far as the others. If Chester tries another "chop-in," Richard will gather up the ball from his position between the infielders and the outfielders and fire it home to try to prevent the winning run from scoring.

Chipper Chester quickly notices the hole in the distant outfield when he steps up to bat. Rifle-Arm Richard had been playing left-center field, and when he moves in, it leaves a sizable gap in the outfield. This is precisely what Chester has been waiting for. He almost licks his lips.

Chester swings with all his might at the first nice pitch he sees. He gets all of it. The ball flies toward left-center field in a rising line drive straight to the gap vacated by Rifle-Arm

Richard. Chester has legitimate reason to expect a home run and game-winning hit.

Chester has not reckoned, however, on the razor-sharp cunning of Wisecrack Wanda. Wanda has watched Chester play softball for several years and has a fairly accurate estimate of Chester's strategies.

As soon as the pitcher had released the ball in his pitch to Chester, Wanda took off in a dead run from her position in left field. Guessing Chester's strategy, she sprinted toward the same gap Chester was aiming for.

Watching the ball as she races toward left-center field, Wanda adjusts her course slightly deeper into the outfield. This is a well-hit ball.

Knowledge of the sheer delight Chipper Chester will take in burning her drives Wisecrack Wanda to an even faster sprint. She pours on all the reserves of speed God has given her. Yet, as the green softball drops out of the sky, Wanda sees she will not quite make it. Further measures are needed.

At precisely the right moment, Wanda's feet leave the ground in an all-out dive. Glove outstretched, Wanda snags the ball, hits the ground and, after rolling a few times, pops up with glove held high, showing the ball to the umpire.

"Owww-oot!" cries Feisty Phil, the fourth-grade boy who is the umpire at the moment. "Annnnd . . . we go to extra innings."

Wisecrack Wanda gently needles Chester as she meets him trotting back to the outfield. "Hey, Slugger, why the sad face?" she asks, commenting on Chester's dejected countenance.

"Oh, it's not because I got out," Chester indignantly replies. "It's just, with all your running around and diving out there, you probably scared off all the rabbits!"

4

BOX SOCIAL

WE FEEL like pioneers.

No, it's not the first time this frontier has been explored, not by a long shot, but it is the first time in my memory.

We are on our way to the box social. The plan is that a few dozen young ladies will bring along a prepared supper-in-a-box. A few dozen young lads will bid for the privilege of eating the meal with the young lady who made it and keeping the box afterward. We lads—herein lies the drama—won't know which lady prepared which box until after we have purchased it.

That is, we're not supposed to know. Later, it appeared a certain Mr. Jason Miller was either very perceptive, very lucky, or he had gathered a bit of intelligence before the auction. Wink, wink.

When we arrive, males and females alike are understandably a bit stiff. Trust our host, Amzie Lehman, and his family to have a solution. Before the auction begins, Amzie randomly divides us into five groups, each with an animal name. We don't know who else is in our group. The crowd forms a circle on the yard outside the basement. When it's time, everyone begins making their animal's sound and looking for the others of their ilk. The race is to be the first to gather your entire group together.

We dogs win. Also, our sounds are convincing enough that the Lehman family's two real dogs come bounding over to join us. So we have the added glory of a pair of mascots. Who let the dogs out anyway?

The atmosphere is now loosened. It's auction time.

When we reenter the basement, the "boxes" have been removed from the anonymous black garbage bags in which they were brought. The array of containers that meets our eyes is a testimony to the creativity of the ladies attending the event.

One girl put her supper in a wooden semi's trailer, a few meals are in toolboxes, and a few are in tackle boxes. The selection also includes a drum, a bridge on a Carrom board, decorated shoeboxes, a bed, a pair of cardboard shoes, a tack bucket, a tack box, and even an LED light with a nice wooden cabinet. These ladies have stepped up to the plate. Plain Janes they are obviously not.

• • •

I have the privilege of conducting the auction tonight, and when we begin, I remind my fellow gentlemen and prospective bidders that boxes are limited, and that while the Lehmans won't let anyone go hungry, boys left without a box will be left to eat in a corner with their ugly buddies. This should be incentive enough, right?

I don't realize it at the time, but the numbers have changed slightly since I was last updated. The number of boys and girls has turned out almost even.

The first box sells for about sixty-five dollars, and we're underway. A few boys get in a bidding war over several boxes, driving one all the way over three hundred dingers. Numerous boxes sell for more than a hundred dollars and the boxes average, I imagine, around a hundred dollars each.

And oh, the two steady boyfriends. I admire their courage for coming here with their girlfriends. They certainly stuck their necks out. All the other bidders know that these boys know which box they want. And all the other bidders are fairly confident these steady boyfriends are not about to quit bidding.

Can you imagine that conversation on the way home? "Well, honey, I wanted to eat with you tonight, but I didn't want to pay quite that much." Yuck.

So the other bidders force the steadies to pay a healthy amount, though they don't go completely beyond reason. They both end up paying between one hundred and two hundred, if memory serves me correctly.

Finally, the auction is over and everyone has a box. Before we eat, Ora Lehman leads us in singing "Come and Dine," and we have prayer.

Then it's time for the moment of truth. We boys sit down with our newly purchased boxes, and the girls who prepared them soon join us. We enjoy the meal and conversation. Amzie and company have a few cerebral activities planned for us after the meal, and Perry Eicher explains The Bridge to us. The Bridge is a charity that reaches out to people with special needs, and that is where the proceeds of tonight's auction are going.

We say our goodbyes then and leave, lighter in pocket but richer in adventures.

5

A SISTER'S LOGIC

DEFINITION OF *hopeless*? Try this: a fourteen-year-old girl is trying to convince her father and three older brothers of her pressing need to spend more time at sleepovers.

The setting is our family supper table, and there is a lively banter going on.

Somewhere in the conversation, Sister Grace utters this priceless quote: "Well, I think sometimes things would go better around here if we'd do them more like I say."

This sentiment is greeted by roars of laughter. Father and brothers ask for permission to take notes on any more precious, forthcoming wisdom.

"No, really." Sis tries again after the guffaws have died down. "We almost never make a decision, like, based on my ideas."

Brother Johnny quickly expresses his wholehearted gratitude for that truth.

Then Father lowers the boom. "Well, in that case, that pony in the barn will have to go. I thought we had her for you, but I guess we don't need her after all."

Cue quick retreat by Grace. "No, no, I do like my little horse."

Round one to the boys.

Sis decides it's time for another sally. "I really think we girls should be allowed to do more sleepovers. You guys just don't know how it is. We just have to go to more sleepovers."

Another roar of laughter issues forth. I challenge Grace to defend that statement, and quickly.

"Well, sleepovers are times that keep us normal," is Sis's reply.

I waste no time attacking the point. "So, are you saying that right now you're abnormal?"

"Well, from being around brothers all the time, I quickly go abnormal," Sister fires back.

Father is again there for the finisher. "Is it a short trip?"

• • •

Debating ability aside, I do admire this younger sister of mine. Whether she is in the barn with her chore boots on or in school with her books, the common theme is a no-nonsense, nose-to-the-grindstone effort.

Grace has several areas where she bests me at her age. She can get more work done with less dawdling than I probably would have. She also earns better grades in school.

They say that you get out of something about what you put in, and this fine sister of mine gives it her best shot. A true lesson for me.

Sister is also a pleasure to be around. Her intensity can be amusing at times, and she also has a fine sense of humor.

• • •

When I see my chance, I express my gratitude for the afore-mentioned conversation around the supper table. "I've got a deadline coming up and I didn't know what I was going to write about, but thanks to you, Grace, I have writing material."

"Oh, no! No! You can't write about me!" Retreat is not fast enough for young sister now. A smoke cloud is thrown up. "You can't write about me. You're not allowed to. You're not allowed to write about people without their permission."

Poking holes in this argument should be fun.

"What about all the people who wrote negative things about, say, President Bush? Do you think they all asked him for permission first?"

"But . . . but . . . he's a president." Little Sister is nearing defeat.

"So what you're saying is, everybody in the United States has the 'right to not be written about' until the moment they become president. Then they lose that right. Is that what you're saying, Grace?"

Father jumps in. "Or if it's not just the president, where do you draw the line? Who all loses that right?"

It is time for Grace to grasp at straws. "Actually, everybody with a salary under one hundred thousand dollars has that right."

Even more eyes roll at this purported logic. Eyes roll, but good humor reigns. Give it up, Sister. Give it up, but try again sometime. This was fun.

6

A BORROWED BIKE AND A WHEELED CHAIR

THESE TWO MEN are poised. They both have a reputation not only for being gifted speakers and successful businessmen, but for having fine senses of humor and enjoying a good joke.

Now the jokes are on them. Is it extra amusing when something funny happens to someone who seems to have his ducks all in a row?

Yep, David Miller of Fish Lake Road and Maynard Yoder of good old State Road 4 are certainly good sports. So, I imagine they won't object if we have a bit of fun at their expense.

David's coming to grief occurred when the weather was warm. I'm quite foggy on the details and therefore will supplement as necessary, but the gist of the story is true. He and his sons combined two of their family's loves—bicycling and canoeing. The happy little group placed their canoes on trailers and pulled them, with their bikes, down the road toward the river. Here is where things began to go awry.

While rolling down the road, happily entertaining thoughts of a peaceful float on the river, a bicycle tire went flat. Rather than returning home, the Millers elected to borrow a bike from a house along the way.

Leaving their own bike there and mounting the borrowed bicycle, the Millers made it uneventfully to the put-in spot.

Now it gets more interesting. In order to prevent the necessity of a return trip to pick up their bicycles, the Millers, as planned, loaded all their gear—including the bicycles, including the *borrowed* bicycle—into their canoes. Slick, right? That way when David and company left the river, they would only need to rig up their trailers once again, mount their bicycles, and pedal home. Ah, the best laid plans . . .

In such a fashion, David and sons entered the river for an enjoyable afternoon of floating with their canoes and their bicycles and the *borrowed* bicycle.

After a short time of serene canoeing, these happy excursionists came upon an obstruction in the water. While attempting to maneuver around a fallen tree, one of the canoes struck another log and, as these treacherous vessels are wont to do, flipped over, depositing all its contents into the river. Person, gear, and bicycle were unceremoniously plopped into the flowing depths.

Chuckle. Yep, it was the borrowed bicycle.

The human occupant—well, former occupant—of the canoe soon clambered out of the water. The gear, though, seemed to lack the same ability to remove itself from its watery hideaway.

So it was up to the men.

David proceeded on Mission Gear Rescue. He was soon able to retrieve the trailer and much of the gear from the murky depths. One item remained lost, however. The bike that belonged to someone else was still somewhere under the muddy water.

Evidently, right in the spot where the canoe had dumped, the river formed a deep pool into which the lost bicycle had fallen. This made retrieving it more difficult.

Time after time, this professional buggy maker and amateur diver plunged headfirst into the river, frantically groping about on the bottom for some hint of a bike. His repeated, unfruitful tries and the frigid water must have been discouraging, but he was in all probability motivated by the thought of returning empty-handed to the owner of the lost bicycle. Imagine *that* conversation.

Eventually another canoeist happened upon this soaking, bedraggled, discouraged Amish man and came to his aid. With the assistance of the stranger, the bike was finally found. The party regrouped and continued down the river, perhaps the worse for wear but better for the adventurous memories.

• • •

Now for Maynard Yoder's, um, adventure. I have even fewer details here, so I'll leave most of it to your imagination.

Hero of story: Amish man.

Background: Something needs to be fixed on the gas light overhead.

Problem: Man can't reach it.

Solution: He stands on a chair.

Next problem: Chair has wheels.

Ending: Man may need MRI on his injured shoulder.

7

SOGGY CYCLING

CYCLISTS COME IN different types. Some bike as a practical matter to save on gas; others bike until their DUI suspension is up; or some bike because they're Amish.

Scott Weisser so categorized bicyclists in a newspaper column. I would fall under the first and last categories there. Obviously I'm Amish, so that explains part of my extensive bike riding, but I also qualify very strongly in the "practical matter" category.

My family calls me a tightwad. I squirm at the idea of paying drivers to go somewhere that is too far or requires too much speed for the horses available at the time. Perhaps I *have* become a bit clingy with my cash.

Take one Friday night, for example. I was invited to a wedding supper located about thirteen miles away. The horses at my disposal were not conditioned well enough for this trip, and it was one of those days when it rains easily.

Because of the rain, I did do some calling around, looking for a "load" going to the wedding. Paying a driver isn't so bad when you've got a whole vanload of people to split the cost.

I found no load, however, and considered skipping the wedding altogether. But I knew the groom well. Plus, weddings are social events, and I do enjoy social events.

At the time I set out, it wasn't raining or I might have been more concerned about the fact that the raincoat only covered me from the waist up.

I had approximately three miles left to go when the rain began. Not just sprinkles, but a decent soaker. With ten miles already put through, I was not about to turn back now. I removed my glasses, pulled up the hood on my raincoat, and continued eastward. These measures, however, did nothing to prevent it raining on the lower half of my body.

• • •

Upon arriving at the wedding and parking my brother Johnny's slick red bicycle, I set off in search of my friends, who had also been invited to the wedding supper. I found them, along with a slew of other young men, in a shop adjacent to the one where the wedding supper was being held.

Metal siding and a metal roof covered this shop where my buddies were hanging out. So the rain may have sounded even worse from in there.

Soon after strolling into the shop, I met up with friend Jason. He married recently, so I don't see him as much anymore. Therefore, Jason makes up for lost time by doubly harassing and making life miserable for me when he gets a chance.

It took only a short minute for Jason to begin working me over.

"So how did you get here?" Jason inquired. This making small talk with an old buddy makes him seem like such a nice guy.

"Bike." I was already slightly wary of the storm to come.

"What! Are you nuts?" Jason's eyebrows shot up, and he began to scan me from head to toe. "Your pants are soaking wet!"

Well done, Sherlock.

"Hey, Lynn! Get over here! This guy biked up here. Can you believe it?" Jason called in backup. Lynn is another recent addition to the ranks of matrimony and is also very much in favor of giving Beachy a hard time.

"You rode a bike up here?" This is Lynn chiming in. "Our church is allowed to have covered buggies."

You could have cut the sarcasm with a knife.

Jason wasn't done yet. "Were you ever desperate to go to a wedding! There must be girls here you're after."

Sherlock Holmes strikes again.

One comfort in all this, though, is that while Lynn and Jason have always been better athletes than I, perhaps I can finally catch up. While Jason and Lynn are becoming plump, sedentary married men, I may yet morph into a lean, mean bicycling machine.

8

A BASS PRO

PLATES CLATTER. Spoons and forks clink. And Mike's eyes twinkle.

The wedding supper has been eaten in this spruced-up shop building north of Shipshewana. Raging appetites have been utterly satiated by the huge variety of food. The plates have been cleared, glasses refilled, and the singing has begun.

Customarily at our weddings, the youth keep their seats after finishing their meal to serenade the bride and groom with a selection of wedding songs. Many times we simple folk just sing the melody, though some enjoy singing in four-part harmony and occasionally do so.

A vanload is here from another Amish community in Vevay, Indiana. They are seated across the table from Mike and are harmonizing nicely.

Now Mike. Michael Lambright is an exceptionally gifted lad. God gave him intelligence, athleticism, charisma, and quick wit. One of his favorite amusements is to act ignorant and see if other people assume he really is. That ignorant, I mean.

Hence the twinkle in his eye. In the pause that follows the second song, Mike flashes a disarming smile at the out-of-towner across the table. "Wow, Philip, nice job! You have a really nice bass voice." Mike pronounces the word *bass* just like the fish—with a short *a*.

Mike keeps his expression deadpan as he watches Philip's eyes widen slightly. The really amusing thing is being able to watch Philip choose a nice way to correct him.

"Thanks, Mike. Uh, you mean *bass*?" Philip pronounces it correctly.

"Oh. Is that how you say it?" Mike is the picture of I-stand-correctedness.

"Well, that's how we usually say it, anyway." Philip lets Mike down easily.

Mike does not bother to correct Philip's impression, instead chuckling on his way home at the thought of the comments in the van as it heads for Vevay.

"He said it how?"

"No!"

"Do these northern Indiana people really not know how to pronounce the four parts?"

• • •

The hook is set even deeper a while later. Mike is traveling with some of the scholars and parents from the school where he teaches. Mike's co-teacher, the bookish, knowledgeable Merlin, sits beside him in the van cruising west on US 20.

And to your left, ladies and gentlemen, is a landmark. The constant flame at the landfill on the south side of US 20 comes into view.

"Hey, everybody!" Mike exclaims. "That is the eternal flame burning as a memorial to President Kennedy."

Mike watches Merlin out of the corner of his eye and almost loses his composure at the sight of Merlin's face going through first shock, then pity, then compassion, as he seeks a way to correct Mike nicely.

"Uh, Mike, I think Kennedy's flame is closer to Washington, DC."

Now Mike has to laugh. A lot. When he regains his breath, he agrees. "Oh yeah, that way it would be closer to where he is buried. That would make sense."

Merlin smiles in chagrin and pulls the hook out of his mouth. This one will sting for a while.

9

THE GIFTED LLOYD YODER

IT'S TWO A.M. on Thanksgiving morning. It's cold. It's rainy. We are out and about. We must be nuts.

The thought of an enjoyable trip to the Dixie Auction in North Carolina makes the weather a little easier to bear. But oh, it's cold!

The driver, Bob, pulls in the driveway in the wee hours. Neighbor Lloyd Yoder is already on board.

Lloyd Yoder raises Belgian draft horses for the strong, deals in ponies for the young, and dispenses a bounteous supply of grief to the weak and innocent. Like me.

Lloyd has made this trip with us in the past, so I have become acquainted with Lloyd. Quite well, actually. I soon realized that it makes Lloyd feel better to verbally harass helpless people. Like me. As a service to the community, I just try to absorb this.

I soon find out that things have not changed much.

We are loading the first of the livestock at the home farm and one of them is Dad's donkey, Myrtle. In appearance, she is like many donkeys, long on ear and short on good looks. Lloyd, on the other hand, is not necessarily short on good looks. He's just short.

Bob, the driver, is a stranger to me and an old friend of Lloyd's. How does Lloyd introduce us? While Lloyd is leading Myrtle the donkey onto the trailer, he says to Bob, while referring to Myrtle, "This is Loren, the one I was telling you about."

Two o'clock in the morning is too early for anything, especially abuse. I can tell this will be a long trip.

When we finally have everything loaded from both our place and Lloyd's, we set off. There are six of us crowded into a Dodge extended cab pickup truck. Driver Bob and his son Dan are in the front along with Lloyd's son Owen, a lad of fifteen. That leaves three of us to cram into the tiny extended cab. I begin the trip on the left side, my dad, David, is in the middle, and Lloyd is in the right corner.

Many of us sleep through the first leg of the trip, and it is fairly peaceful. We stop for breakfast in Ohio, then point our noses southward on Interstate 77. The country becomes more rugged. The trailer is loaded down heavily and the truck labors up inclines, sometimes slowing to thirty miles an hour.

We make a fuel stop in Virginia. It is almost sixty degrees and the warmer air feels like springtime to Indiana's winter.

Here I make a mistake. When we climb back into the cab to continue the trip, I end up in the middle of the back seat. This new position restricts movement even more and may even have less legroom. After a while, I become uncomfortable.

I begin squirming occasionally. Sometimes I even stand up, as much as one can in such limited space, to relieve the growing ache. I even complain a few times. Lloyd shows little sympathy for me.

It is about this time that Lloyd's wife, Martha, calls. Lloyd is talking on a borrowed cell phone and catching up on the latest when he begins to fill Martha in on the details of the trip. They get to the subject of my current discomfort. Lloyd pretends to be oblivious to the fact that I am sitting right beside him and my ear is about twenty-four inches from his mouth.

Lloyd is speaking. "It is high time Loren grew up and realized you can't always have everything exactly as you want it." Waves of brotherly love emanate from him.

• • •

We finally arrive at the fairgrounds where the Dixie Auction is held. We unload, unhook the trailer, and take off for Statesville. We find a Shoney's to get a meal before Dad and I are dropped off at the hotel. Bob, Dan, Lloyd, and Owen plan to camp out at the sale.

Before we order at Shoney's, Dad and Lloyd spot the buffet bar. According to signage, it's closed. Dad and Lloyd order it anyway and somehow get away with it. The rest of us order conventionally.

As soon as the waitress leaves, the two hotshots go load up on mashed potatoes, gravy, and many other things they find on the buffet bar. They then bring their food back to the table where the rest of us are still waiting for our food like good little boys. The two early birds take great pleasure in pronouncing their food satisfying while we others sit there becoming hungrier by the minute.

Throughout the rest of the trip, Dad or Lloyd will occasionally rub this incident under our noses again. Lloyd once commented, "And the worst part is, we only paid five bucks." Most of us paid almost twice that for our supper.

You've got to hand it to Lloyd, though. The man is gifted. Who else could deal out so much harassment and grief and actually make the recipient like it?

10

LLOYD YODER REPRISE

Aʜ, ɪᴛ'ꜱ ᴛʜᴇ ꜰʀɪᴅᴀʏ after Thanksgiving. It is Black Friday to some. To me it's Happy Friday. We're at the Dixie Auction, and one of the most activity-filled days of the year for me as an auctioneer is about to start.

My first assignment is a semitrailer loaded with tack. We start selling, and selling fast. The boss, Dean Beachy, has little patience for a dawdling auctioneer. So, we roll. Four or five other auction rings start at the same time we do.

Around noon, Dean sends me inside to sell saddles and harnesses. This is a real adventure.

The inside ring is loaded with people crowding around the wagon where the saddles and harnesses are displayed. People are in the grandstands and bidding from there. There are even people behind the auction block where I am sitting.

There are three or four ringmen on the wagon, and there's a ringman on the ground as well as one on the block. Sometimes three or four of them are shouting in bids at the same time. It's challenging, it's fast-paced, and it's crazy. I love it. Roll on.

I sell for a while until I am relieved by Atlee Shetler of Ohio. He gives me a nice break, and then I sell until it is almost time for carriages at three o'clock.

This time I am replaced by the reigning national champion auctioneer, Eli Detweiler Jr., of North Carolina. He has a way of chanting that is extremely fast and yet as clear as a bell. The man can sell.

After carriages, it's time for a horse sale. One hundred and fifty will be sold tonight, followed by six or seven hundred tomorrow. Dad's two horses and one of Lloyd's ponies will be sold tonight, and Dad's donkey and twenty-five of Lloyd's ponies tomorrow. Yes, we had a full trailer on the way down here.

I jump in the ring along with some other ringmen, and the horse sale begins. The two horses my dad, David Beachy, brought down fetch $2,300 each. Dad is pleased. Lloyd's pony doesn't do as well, but there is a better day coming tomorrow.

• • •

The following morning the horse sale gets under way at eight o'clock. Dean sets a rapid pace as is expedient if you have six hundred horses to sell in one day.

At ten o'clock Atlee Shetler and I head outside to sell the remainder of the tack on the semitrailer. That takes a few hours but it's a sunny day, and, guess what, we sell fast.

Twenty-five Yoder ponies and one Beachy donkey later, our work here is finished and we head north, homeward, on Interstate 77.

• • •

This is the time, with six of us crowded into the cab of one pickup truck, that we start rehashing the events of the past few days. Things that happened are discussed, along with things that might have happened, things that could have happened, and things that should have happened.

Then a call comes in for Lloyd. It is his wife, Martha. Lloyd begins to fill her in on the selling prices of their animals. Unfortunately for Lloyd, he has a committee of five editors that can hear every word he's saying and would be happy to straighten Lloyd out should he begin to err in his retelling.

Lloyd is telling his wife how their team of gray ponies sold. "They brought five or six hundred, which is okay, but they should have brought more . . ."

I begin to guffaw in the opposite corner. I think Lloyd is getting a bit greedy. It is high time I get in a few licks in this one-sided battle of wits.

Lloyd is not down for long. When he hears me chuckling at him, he does just what an old military general would do: Attack, always attack.

He abruptly shifts direction and heads into the realm of fiction. "But you know, we think we're doing good if we make five dollars. The Beachys are walking around with hankies wiping tears, because their mare only brought twenty-three hundred and they really had no money in her."

11

THE KANSAS ANDY BOYS' GOOD DEED

THEIR SENSE OF HUMOR is legendary—and quirky. Stories are told far and wide of their tongue-in-cheek pranks. And yet, often the instigators themselves will do no more than crack a slight smile. It's the onlookers who will be roaring out loud. They are the Kansas Andy Boys.

These inimitable men grew up in Kansas, the first arena for their wide array of practical jokes. The stories, however, have drifted back to the Hoosier State and are passed around with relish.

• • •

The crew goes sneaking down the dirt road late on a Friday night, looking for the gate to Corncob Calvin's cows. The plan is to open the gate to the pasture and herd the sleepy Holsteins onto the road. The boys—Sammy, Mose, and Henry—feel fairly safe since a passing car is a rare occurrence.

The brothers open the gate and, with a bit of encouragement, the thirty cows are soon sufficiently scattered along the road, enjoying the fresh grazing and waking up fast.

It's Henry's turn. He runs up to the door of the farmhouse fast enough that he is out of breath when he pounds on the door. Being breathless is part of the plan.

Henry pounds on the door with enough urgency that the sleeping farmer wakes in just a few minutes. He comes to the door, groggy and with trepidation. There are only a few reasons someone would pound on his door at 11:30 p.m., and none of them are good.

Corncob Calvin soon recognizes the puffing form of the lad from the next section over.

"What's the matter, Henner?"

"Did you know your cows are out and grazing along the road?" Henry inquires, all concern now.

"Oh, no," groans the farmer. "I'll get my boots and be right out." This will mean waking his reluctant wife, running around on the road chasing frisky cows, and perhaps fixing the fence before seeing his warm bed again.

Henry comforts him, though. "My two brothers and I will stay and help you get them back in."

When the farmer and his half-awake wife come stumbling down the driveway to the road, they are much relieved to see three husky, straight-faced boys available to assist with the chasing. The youngsters even generously offer to go through the pasture and loop around the cows in order to surround the now frisky bovines.

"You two just stay here and don't let them get past you," the energetic lads instruct Calvin and his yawning wife.

Three young men slip under the barbed wire fence and go bounding around the far end of the herd. In a few moments the group of cows reverses direction and is hustled back toward the resident farmers. With the resolute couple forming a barricade across the escape route ahead of them and three shouting lads behind, the cows have little choice but to file reluctantly back into their pasture.

"Wow, is that ever a relief," sighs Corncob Calvin as he latches the chain on the gate. "This could have been a long night. Thank you, boys, so much for all your help."

"Yes, I don't know what we would have done without you!" gushes Calvin's wife. "You boys must come in for a snack since we're all awake now anyway."

The lads, eyes twinkling only slightly, quickly accept and are treated to tea, milk, and some delicious cookies in the farmers' kitchen as a repayment for their kind, generous deed.

PART II

Winter

12

IF YOU GET OUT OF YOUR BUGGY, GET READY TO RUN

CHILDREN, DO NOT try this with your horse (or pony or any live animal). Results may vary, and they could certainly be much more devastating than the ones Freeman Gingerich reaped when he attempted the stunt.

My friend Freeman of rural Shipshewana is no dummy. He has many bright ideas and intelligent insights and, what's more rare, the ambition to apply them. He is human, though, and it has been proven before—sometimes smart people do dumb things.

Freeman lives north of town and works west of it on busy US 20.

Freeman is on his way to work on a frosty winter morning. With the extra chilly temperatures and stiff western wind today, he has elected to drive his horse and buggy. Riding his bicycle would bring the advantage of stimulation and would likely deliver him to work wide-awake. But this morning it is just too cold. Freeman hitches Ranger to the buggy.

The relatively warm interior of the buggy and the rhythmic cadence of Ranger's hoofs do cause a problem. Freeman is beset by drowsiness. He tries opening the front, he tries shaking himself, but after a few minutes he catches his head nodding again.

It surely won't do to fall asleep while driving. He is a mile and a half north of busy US 20 and wants to be alert when he gets to the highway.

Inspiration strikes. Freeman thinks of a sure way to wake up. If he gets out of the buggy and runs alongside for a bit, it will get his blood pumping and infuse him with a dose of oxygen. Ranger doesn't trot all that rapidly anyway, and Freeman figures he can easily jog beside the buggy while keeping one hand on Ranger's lines. After jogging for a stimulating half mile or so, he will simply hop back into the driver's seat and be wide-awake for the highway portion of his trip. Brilliant. Right?

"Whoa, Ranger."

Ranger is not accustomed to stopping in the middle of the road, but he waits obligingly while Freeman climbs out and rearranges the lines to his liking.

"Giddap, Ranger."

Ranger feels his load is a bit lighter and hears an extra set of feet pounding behind him. In his early days, this would have spooked him, but he has covered too many miles to be alarmed by little things now. He trots along at his usual pace.

Freeman is fast waking up. This is fun. His left hand stays on the lines while his right arm pistons alongside as he trots along with Ranger. The narrow country road doesn't allow Freeman room to run on the asphalt, but the gravel shoulder is firm enough for a decent running surface.

Suddenly things go wrong. Freeman is later unsure if he stepped on a loose rock, if his foot hit something solid, or if he simply tripped over his own feet. Something though, goes alarmingly awry with his running gear, and Freeman goes sprawling face-first into the gravel.

The lines slip out of Freeman's hand and Ranger trots on, oblivious to the extra commotion.

Freeman would like to gingerly check himself over for injuries now, but he does not have that luxury. His airplane is beelining for US 20 with no pilot.

After clambering to his feet and inadvertently groaning a bit, Freeman sets out at a brisk trot after his horse. A brisk trot will not suffice, Freeman soon sees, and breaks into an all-out sprint. Legs pumping, eyes bugging, and breath tearing, Freeman makes some quick calculations. He's not going to catch up. Ranger, though his pace is still methodical, simply has too big a head start.

Thinking quickly, Freeman turns into a driveway, barrels up to the shop, snatches a bicycle, and, legs churning and gravel flying, sets out in fresh pursuit. He'll explain to the owners of the bicycle later.

Trying to catch up before Ranger reaches the highway is a long-lost cause, though. Freeman can only cringe from a thousand feet behind while Ranger slows down as accustomed and makes a right turn onto US 20. Thankfully no traffic nails the rig, and Ranger sets out westward for the last mile of his journey to Hilltop Machine Shop, Freeman's workplace.

When Freeman turns the corner one long minute later, he immediately realizes the brisk headwind will add to his difficulties. He has to struggle for every pump of the pedals now, and his speed is actually reduced.

Oblivious to Freeman's struggles, Ranger trots on, covering the familiar mile at his usual pace, breezing through the next crossroad and climbing the long hill to Hilltop Machine Shop. Now tired from the climb, Ranger turns in at the usual driveway, trots up to the barn, and stops. There he waits patiently until his owner catches up and unhitches him.

After Freeman has tied his trusty steed in the barn, his breath finally slows down though his hands are still a bit trembly. He shakes his head once, thanks God for watching over him and his horse, grabs his lunch box off the buggy, and heads to the shop to go to work.

Freeman has accomplished one goal this morning. He is now wide awake.

13

SPELLING BEE JITTERS

THEY HAVE STUDIED, sweated, fretted, visualized, pronounced, practiced, and dreamed for weeks over a six-page list of words. Now the day is here. Our district's eighth graders, thirty-some students representing approximately a dozen schools, have gathered for an old-fashioned spelldown. And they are nervous.

Vans arrive and disgorge teachers, parents, and children. Horses trot in, tugging their black carriages, and are tied at the hitching rack or stabled in the older, sprawling barn whose crimson color matches that of the new shop building adjacent to it where the people are gathering and where the bee is to be held.

Inside the shop, we shed our jackets and exchange pleasantries with our acquaintances. Well, the adults do. Right now the teenage spellers look rather stiff and aren't conversing much. In fact, if some enterprising electric company were to attach their batteries to this bunch, collectively, the nerves could light up Chicago.

Memories of my own spelling bees come back as we get set to begin. Nerve-stricken, my classmate misspelled *mop* in the practice round. He did not realize it until he returned to the lineup and a fellow student informed him.

"Baker, you said *o-m-p*."

"Oh."

The young adults assembled today are all about fourteen though, and possibly a bit more poised than Adam Baker was at eleven.

Poised, yes. And intelligent, too. Through the afternoon, it will become apparent that they have a sound knowledge of these words. The winner, however, rather than being the one with the highest IQ, the superior memory, or even the best study habits, may be the individual who can best steady his or her nerves.

Kenny V. Miller, also known as Six-Foot Kenny, and his wife, Edna, are hosting us today. Kenny gets everyone seated. The students are on benches in the center of the assembly. Their parents and teachers are to their left and right. The judges, David Yoder, Ray Wingard, and Lori Wingard, preside from a table at the front. I, acting as the pronouncer today, am seated at the end of the judge's table.

Kenny leads us in prayer and in singing "Amazing Grace." He goes through the rules briefly. It's time.

The spellers stand and form a ring around the room. This wheel rotates slowly as the words are spelled. An eighth-grade lady from Blue Ridge leads things off.

We make it through the practice round with only a few nervous missteps. Then we begin our run for the roses in earnest. Many words are spelled correctly, but a few are not, and the number begins dwindling. Discussing it later, the talking heads agree that most of the eliminated spellers are perfectly able to spell the words but simply made nervous mistakes.

Like Joshua Hochstetler. This Plainview eighth grader is later incredulous that he put an *e* on the end of *saliva*. So it goes. He'll probably never forget it.

One young lady from Forks Valley has plenty of presence of mind, though, to keep the pronouncer on his toes. *Species* is her word, and the pronouncer gives it to her. "Species," she repeats, but pronounces it differently. She proceeds to spell it correctly, pronounce it her way again, and retake her place in the line. The pronouncer, curious, circles the word and looks it up when there is a break. Yep, the girl was right. *Species* has a *sh* sound in the middle.

Finally we get down to six contestants. We take a break and the rules change. Now, in order to eliminate a speller, the next speller must correctly spell the misspelled word.

We grind on. A few more fine spellers drop out, and finally only two remain: a girl from Plainview and my own lone eighth grader. Much to her chagrin, my student soon trips up and only puts one *r* in the middle of *warrior*. Plainview's pupil pounces and becomes the champion.

The three top spellers are allowed to choose a brand new storybook as their prize. We're not much for trophies.

The real trophy, though, the true prize? It's the memories, friend, the memories. Lord willing, years later they'll be telling their children, "Yeah, the spelling bee was at Six-Foot Kenny's in my eighth-grade year. I knew every one of those words and there were only a few of us left. I couldn't believe I put an *e* on the end of *saliva* . . ."

14

WISECRACK WANDA

ARRIVING AT SCHOOL, she strolls from the bike rack to the schoolhouse, stray strands of hair fluttering rebelliously outside her covering. The hair, though, shouts not so much of rebellion but of a relaxed attitude about perfection, or the lack of it. Here is the story of Wisecrack Wanda, who has a tendency to alternately render me helpless in peals of mirth and frustrate me to the point of pulling my hair out.

Walking in a relaxed manner, even a slight slouch, toward the schoolhouse, she carries her lunch pail, which is swinging like a pendulum. Wanda stops to observe some of her fellow scholars engaging in an energetic snow fight prior to the morning bell. Wanda happily shouts encouragement to the snowy participants. She points out one unlucky boy's resemblance to Frosty the Snowman, cheerily asking him if he bit off more than he could chew. The boys holler back, offering grave threats of face-washings and the like the moment Wanda chooses to enter the fray.

Wisecrack Wanda is well known by all the pupils here at Sunrise Valley School. She is known for her ability to come up with smart cracks at the drop of a hat, as well as for her lax attitude about the minor details of life. Details like keeping her hair neatly combed and getting all the dirt off the floor when sweeping the schoolhouse—they are of small consequence to Wanda.

The boys at school are quite fond of Wanda. Her keen wit and rib-splitting comebacks help her fit right in with the boys in their friendly bantering. Tomboy characteristics flash through occasionally. Whether it's exchanging threats of imminent face-washings in winter, or informing the boys in no uncertain terms that she's going to burn them once she gets up to bat during softball games when the weather is warmer, Wanda can hold her own when it comes to trash talk.

Wanda also possesses the athletic ability to back up many of her threats. Though slender as a sapling, Wanda can be seen hitting screaming line drives over the infield or leaping to catch a softball almost beyond her reach. She puts her God-given athletic ability to use to give an unsuspecting boy a faceful of snow when the situation demands. Behind the feisty façade, however, lurks a kind heart—a heart that endears Wanda to her classmates. A willingness to reach out and be friends with those less fortunate helps Wanda to be held in high esteem with the girls at Sunrise Valley.

• • •

One chilly noon recess on the snow-covered playground of Sunrise Valley School, pupils gathered to play a game called Ten Eskimos. The five "itters," one of whom was Wanda, gathered at the jail in the middle of the playground. All other pupils scattered, knowing if the "itters" tagged them, they would be required to stand in the frigid jail. To get the game underway, all the "itters" shouted in unison, "One, two, three, GO!"

Karl, a first grader, enjoying his "free" status, made the mistake of needling Wanda. "Go? Where shall I go?" he inquired, chuckling at his own wit. Wanda, still in an easy trot outward from the jail, turned her attention to the now concerned offender. In a flash, it was all over as Wanda turned her prolific physical and mental abilities on at the same time. In a few quick strides she caught up with Karl. As she tagged him, she retorted, "Go? Go to jail! Go directly to jail! Do not pass Go. Do not collect two hundred dollars."

15

THAT GILLIGAN CAN RUN

HE LIED. He died."

That is the story of Ananias and Sapphira as told by Gung Ho Gilligan, a first grader.

Every Monday morning for devotions at school, students take turns sharing what they heard in church or discussed in devotions the day before. Gung Ho Gilligan heard the story of Ananias and Sapphira and proceeded to share his very concise version of it.

Gung Ho Gilligan is experiencing first grade with inimitable gusto. He has watched five older siblings make their way through school and it is finally his turn. With the benefit of so many brothers' and sisters' experiences to guide him, he is quite confident he knows the answers to some of the perplexing problems first grade offers.

This confidence, combined with a well-trained work ethic, fuels an eyes-on-the-prize, forget-all-distractions way of getting things done. Gilligan zeroes in on answers like a fat pony on a carrot.

If Gilligan is introduced to a new word that sounds almost like one he already knows, it must be the same one. Never mind the bothersome difference of a few consonant sounds. Close enough. The carrot is devoured.

When Gung Ho Gilligan and his four classmates sounded out the word *sum* for the first time, I asked them what it meant. We had discussed it in math class a few times, so there was a chance they would know. *Sum*, however, sounded way too close to another word that Gilligan already knew. When called upon to tell the class what a *sum* was, Gilligan straightaway pointed to the shortest digit on his hand, his *thumb*.

Also, according to Gilligan, the opposite of *dim* is *fat*.

While some of Gilligan's fellow seven-year-olds sometimes have trouble shutting out distractions and focusing on the task at hand, Gilligan has no such issues. Once he picks up his pencil or "recognizes" a word, he is locked in. He can taste the carrot already.

Gung Ho Gilligan's sister, Wisecrack Wanda, is a world-wise eighth grader and can't help but roll her eyes at some of Gilligan's utterances. Wanda is a voracious reader and an English whiz. Proper grammar comes somewhat naturally for her.

Little brother Gilligan, while also possessing a bright, quick mind, has not had the benefit of much reading on his own. His grammar is a bit shaky at times. When Gilligan was asked to use the word *sat* in a sentence, he was completely willing. After all, he knew perfectly well what it meant. "We are *satting* on a bench," he quickly composed. Right about then Wanda had a coughing fit at her desk.

The bull's-eye approach carries over to the playground for Gung Ho Gilligan. Once he knows where he wants to go, what sense is there in dawdling around? The pedal is stomped flat and Gilligan makes a beeline for the goal.

• • •

We are playing softball. Gilligan has just beat out a single and it is my turn to bat. I smack one deep into the outfield. It could be a triple or even a home run. So I hustle for first base, intending to get as far as I can. Gung Ho Gilligan takes off for second. His legs are much shorter than mine, and he only has a lead of about fifty-four feet.

Gilligan knows where he needs to go, though, and intends to do his best to stay in front of the much bigger base runner behind him. He turns on the jets. His short legs work like pistons.

Gung Ho Gilligan, all of four feet tall, steams around third and scoots across home plate safely. Resting on third, I hear an admiring comment float in from an opposing third grader playing the outfield.

"I mean, that Gilligan can *run*."

16

WINDY WILLY'S HOT AXE

THE CLATTER of dishes stops. The womenfolk pause from their chore of washing the supper dishes. Quickly wiping their hands on towels or aprons, the ladies hurry to the living room where the men are already leaning forward in their chairs with gleams of anticipation in their eyes. The children cease their noisy clatter and turn to see what has the adults so enthralled. They, too, are soon caught up in the tale. Windy Willy is telling another story.

"Yessirree, I was hauling manure last Saturday, cleaning away that big pile behind the barn, you know? I was a little slow in the morning 'til I had all the stiffness out of my joints, but I tell you, once I warmed up, I really made that shovel fly. Why, once I'd get done spreading one load on the field, I'd have another loaded and back to the field so fast I had to wait to start spreading it 'til all the manure from the first load had hit the ground."

This fantastic tale is met with hearty guffaws and a few rolling eyes from an appreciative audience.

Willy's neighbor and dear friend Benny Mast, who is used to these tall tales, slyly remarks, "Yeah, Willy, if everyone was like you, the skid loader companies would go out of business in a hurry."

"They sure would, and the wood splitter companies too." Windy Willy is unruffled by his neighbor's sarcasm. "Did I ever tell you what happened a few weeks ago when I was in the woods splitting firewood?"

"No, do tell," chuckles Benny, settling in for another round of entertainment.

• • •

Windy Willy is a local legend. His far-fetched stories are often repeated over campfires and at other social gatherings. These tales are passed down from father to son, but unlike other stories, these do not become exaggerated. They are already stretched to the max. The stories come right off the press like that.

While truth is hard to find in Windy Willy's tales, entertainment abounds.

Many is the time when a toiling farmer will pause in his work, wipe the sweat from his brow, and say with a twinkle in his eye, "You know, this reminds me of a Windy Willy story . . ."

• • •

But now, it is time for fresh material straight from Windy Willy himself. The audience collectively resists the urge to rub their hands together as Willy begins the wood-splitting story.

The wrinkles on Windy Willy's face and the heavy gray in his hair betray his age. However, there is a youthful gleam in Windy Willy's eyes that makes one forget the fact that Willy is well past middle age.

"Yep, I was splitting firewood and got good and warmed up. The chips were flying pretty good, but my axe kept getting too hot to keep using. I was prepared for this, though, and had an extra axe that I used while I laid the first one in the ditch to cool off. I kept splitting through the forenoon in this manner, switching axes, always keeping one axe in the water to cool while I used the other one. I didn't think much of this, as it's not that unusual for me. Guess I didn't really realize just how fast I was going 'til I stopped and went to the house for lunch. My eyes just about popped out of my head when I saw what the neighbors were doing."

Here Windy Willy pauses for dramatic effect. He is a polished storyteller.

"They were butchering hogs. Where do you think they were scalding the carcasses? That's right—the same ditch where I was cooling my hot axes!"

17

AUCTIONS AND PRANKS

THE HORSE MARKET is thriving. So is the Amish community's love of fun and fellowship. These were both evidenced by a quick trip to Cloverdale, Indiana, one weekend.

We set out in the wee hours of Friday morning. The other five goobers, Richard Slabach, LaVern Hershberger, Dave Hochstetler, Joe Lambright, and the driver, Sonny Beachey, were already on board when they picked me up.

Richard and I shared a seat for this trip and slept most of the way south until we stopped for breakfast near Indianapolis.

Inside the family-style restaurant, I left the full table for just a few minutes. Mistake.

When I returned, there was a foreign substance floating in my coffee that looked suspiciously like black pepper. After a short, quick interrogation of the five suspects, my deductions pointed toward LaVern Hershberger even though a few of these highly innocent goofballs expressed the likelihood that it was only coffee grounds floating in my precious drink.

Smile. This could be a fun weekend. Just remember, boys, the pen is mightier than the black pepper. And you started it.

• • •

We arrive at the C Bar C Expo Center just outside Cloverdale at midmorning—in plenty of time for the tack sale at noon and stallion presentation at three o'clock.

This leaves plenty of time to relax and catch up with old friends. I speak with a few of my Ohio cousins as well as friends from Pennsylvania and Illinois. Auctioneer buddy David Miller from Ohio is here, and we have time to chat for a bit.

I only plan to spot bids at this auction. Therefore, it's not necessary for me to do much preparatory work. It is a relaxing time.

The horse auction begins at five o'clock with David handling the gavel. We soon realize that horses are in demand as they sell well throughout this Friday evening portion of the auction. The real highlights are likely to come during tomorrow's auction, though.

The auction is over in plenty of time for the fun and games to begin. Four volleyball nets are set up in the sale ring and are filled in short order with leaping, grunting, young Amish men.

Many more, mostly older and not so athletically inclined, lounge on the seats on each side of the nets. After a bit of volleyball, I join them. Just because they're not playing volleyball here in the seats doesn't mean it's boring. Stories are being told, acquaintances are being renewed, and some good-natured ribbing is taking place. I sit with LaVern, Dave, and Reuben Schrock of Illinois.

Reuben is one of those classic personalities. He seems to know everyone from almost everywhere and has a good story or three to tell about many of them.

The evening progresses. Things get (almost) a bit silly. Before long, someone gets after Richard to do his well-known motorcycle imitation. We bring him the microphone. Kenny Hochstetler brings him a Pepsi, and he finally agrees after three of us sit in a row in front of him so he can hide. Reuben makes sure Dave is one of the three. Reuben says Dave can cover up a lot more space than he can.

At last, the anticipated moment arrives. The sound of a motorcycle comes blaring from the speakers. Volleyball players turn and gaze around, trying to find the source of the sound. A dog yips. Laughter erupts. The resemblance to a real motorcycle is uncanny.

Somehow Kenny Hochstetler of Topeka, Indiana, and Oba Hershberger of Illinois end up with the mike. Now there are two nuts in a shell. They sit beside each other on the folding chairs, each egging the other on.

Oba and Kenny end up singing a song. Oba's is a beautiful original one and Kenny's involves yodeling, though he has trouble remembering the second line.

So the evening is going when our load leaves for the hotel. I take some cold medicine before turning in for the night. I'd like my voice to be in good shape for tomorrow.

• • •

Saturday morning dawns windy, cold, and snowy in Cloverdale, Indiana. We're glad the horse sale today is to be in a heated building.

Our load—LaVern, Richard, Dave, Joe, driver Sonny, and yours truly—leaves the hotel in time to eat breakfast before we need to be at the auction.

We find a truck-stop-slash-family-restaurant for breakfast, order our food, and wait. The establishment is doing a booming business this morning, largely because of the horse sale, and it seems perhaps the cooks are having a difficult time keeping up. Some begin to lament the long wait, but it does give us an opportunity to chat.

Our drinks arrive, though, and I have not forgotten the black pepper floating in my coffee twenty-four hours ago. Heh, heh. Furthermore, I'm sitting at a table facing the prime suspect.

It does not appear, though, as if LaVern has any intention of leaving the table and giving me an opportunity to return the favor. He is too cagey for that.

I peer around him toward the kitchen. "Does that lady back there look like your wife?"

Men have such blind spots where their wives are concerned. LaVern turns around and looks for a long time. Evidently he misses his wife.

When he turns back around, LaVern soon notices all the flecks floating in his orange juice. "You sap," he mutters, but the sheepish grin on his face is evidence of his good humor.

The food is delicious when it arrives, and we make it to the C Bar C Expo Center in plenty of time for the Dutch Harness Horse Sale taking place there today.

• • •

Horse sales for the Amish community provide not only economic activities but a time of fellowship, catching up, and having fun.

Committee men Andrew Gingerich, Melvin Gingerich, and LaMar Schrock have done a nice job of organizing this sale, and it goes off smoothly. Dale Chupp of Shipshewana, Indiana, and David Miller of Dundee, Ohio, handle the gavel, and nine other bid-spotters and I rotate through the ring.

There seems to be a demand for horses, and they sell well today. Miss Independence is the first horse in the sale ring this morning, and this four-year-old daughter of Sandokan rings the bell for $9,500 and ends up topping the sale.

Other horses sell well too, with only a handful of no-sales in this two-day auction.

18

THE WHITEBOARD WARS

IT LOOKS INCONSPICUOUS, that little whiteboard does. It only measures about eight inches by twelve and hangs beside the door to the kitchen.

There have been some mighty battles fought on this smooth white surface, though. After the addition of the little white bulletin board, we quickly became aware of how many wise guys there are in our family.

The idea was noble enough. Mom wanted an organized way of knowing where her youngsters were planning to spend the weekend. With five of us scattering hither and yon to different friends' houses each weekend, it is small wonder she had a hard time keeping track of who was here and who was where.

Hence the whiteboard. Each child over the age of sixteen had his or her name written on the whiteboard, and beside our name was inscribed our planned destination for the weekend. Simple enough, right? Not in this family. Uh-uh.

The first week the whiteboard was put to use, I was planning to be at home. Simply writing "here" on the board would just not do, though. That's boring. My destination was shown as "1600 Pennsylvania Avenue."

Brother Johnny wrote "here and there" beside his name. For a guy with his wit, I thought it was pathetic. I told him so. I mean, Babe Ruth isn't famous for hitting infield singles. Brother Johnny rose to the occasion the next week. Now his destination was shown as "state of delusion."

This was mildly amusing, but I laughed out loud the next morning when I saw what was inscribed right under it. Next to Sister Grace's name was "state of confusion."

This is a pretty apt description of where Grace purports to spend much of her time. Her standby line after a slightly sophisticated joke that leaves everyone else laughing is, "I am confused." She just doesn't get it. It's actually rather endearing. But evidently she's comfortable with that, because we later found out it was she herself who wrote the "state of confusion" crack on the board.

Cream rises to the top, and a superior wisecracker soon surfaced. Sister Ramah is employed at home in the barn. She stays fairly busy there—much to her chagrin. This prompted her to write on the board for her destination: "Duh, the barn."

Her chores do not occupy her active mind, however, and she has all day to plot her next whiteboard assault.

Ramah's attacks come with typical feminine ferocity and once prompted her oldest brother (um, me) to note his destination thus: "Here, within reach of the resident thirteen-year-old who fell from the smart aleck tree and didn't miss a branch on the way down."

She's actually fourteen and becomes aggravated when one accuses her of being a "typical thirteen-year-old." Yes, she's fourteen and feisty and therefore ideal to pick on. Occasionally she is waiting for me with a loaded cannon.

As I was gently needling—well, needling, anyway—my youngest sister, Susann, Ramah stepped into the room and called me an "arrogant, overweight, stiff-necked, male chauvinist pig."

Other than that, I'm a real teddy bear.

Well, Ramah has now attacked my gender.

As the whiteboard war continued, it was time to crank the intensity up a notch. The next time I was planning to be home, I inscribed "Here—*sans* feminine encumberment."

It was like attacking a bear with a butter knife. Soon my entry was erased and replaced with, "The perpetual bacheloristic state of lonesomeness caused by ignorance of feminine charms."

Grace was confused. I was defeated.

That is, until the next week.

19

THE PEN IS MIGHTIER THAN THE BREAKFAST BURRITO

IT IS DARK and snowy in Flagstaff, Arizona. Not that the other two fearless explorers are noticing.

We are on vacation, and farther south than home according to latitude and longitude. The temperatures right now, though, feel a lot like Goshen, Indiana. Isn't Arizona supposed to be warm?

It's New Year's Eve, 7:35 p.m. I'm sitting in a hotel room writing, while two of my comrades are sleeping on the beds to my right. Four friends and I are on this western trip during our Christmas vacation. I will certainly try not to bore you.

DECEMBER 24

We take a train from Elkhart to Chicago. *We* means my four friends and I. Actually, I think I'll give you their names. It would be a shame to wake them up just to ask for permission. We are Ivan Miller, Freeman Bontrager, Myron Miller, Glenn Yoder, and yours truly.

During our layover in the Windy City, we enjoy a visit to the Willis (formerly Sears) Tower Skydeck. After coming back to

Union Station, we board the train, the California Zephyr, and at about 2:00 p.m. we head west.

We notice that our train car attendant, a middle-aged lady, has a habit of calling people "sweetness." This is new to us country boys and causes some amusement in our camp. Soon, Ivan is calling all of us "sweetness." Ivan is a dear friend of mine who arranged much of this trip for us. He has a delightful sense of humor, as you will yet find out.

I tell you, this is a rough life. Soon after pointing our noses westward, we grab our Rook cards and stroll down to the lounge car for a card game. We relax at a table where we have a splendid view of the passing countryside. We also have fetched plenty of food to munch on while enjoying the smooth train ride and a spirited card game. Ten days of this! How will I ever last through it? Ahhh . . .

DECEMBER 25

It's Christmas Day and the Rocky Mountains are coming up! We have time to stretch our legs in Denver before chugging toward the Rockies.

Today we see many of God's scenic masterpieces. How great Thou art!

At Glenwood Springs, Colorado, we have a little time to get off the train. I go inside, wanting to make a phone call. I am only getting started when I hear two blasts from the train's whistle. Turns out the phone call isn't necessary after all. Beachy doesn't waste much time getting back to his train. It would have been a long time before Late Loren would have heard the end of it, had he missed the train and been stuck in Colorado.

DECEMBER 26

The end of the first leg of the journey has arrived! We get off the train in Emeryville, California. A bus takes us to adjacent San Francisco.

We cross the San Francisco Bay on a large bridge. Myron and I think it almost has to be the Golden Gate Bridge, because of its resemblance to pictures we have seen. The other three boys are not so sure, and we do not reach an agreement. The debate remains at an impasse for the night, which we spend at a hotel in San Francisco, as we think it is probably too late to tour the city.

DECEMBER 27

Early this morning we hire a taxi to drive us to the bus stop. This presents an opportunity to settle the debate of the night before. The taxi driver says it is not the Golden Gate Bridge we crossed but the Bay Bridge. You would think he should know better, working right there close to it like he does. The funny thing is that a map we received from the hotel also showed this bridge to be the Bay Bridge and not the Golden Gate, which is across town.

Myron and I think we ought to call the mapmakers and politely ask them to correct their map. No telling how many people they have misled by getting it wrong like this.

Yosemite National Park is our next destination.

DECEMBER 27

"Hey, sweetness, this breakfast burrito sure is tasty. What is it like, not having a breakfast burrito?"

Ivan is asking for trouble again. He makes comments something like this to amuse himself, cause us grief, and shorten the days for us all.

We are on a California Amtrak train from Emeryville, California, en route to Merced, California. There, we plan to catch a bus to that beautiful national park—Yosemite.

My four traveling companions have just returned from the food car, where they purchased something for breakfast. For some reason or other, I decided not to get something right away.

Now these friends of mine are just having a blast rubbing in the fact that they have food and I don't. The pen is mightier than the breakfast burrito, boys.

California is a beautiful place containing a wide variety of landscapes. This morning we pass through vast fields of fertile farmland. After boarding the bus in Merced, the country soon becomes hilly and more rugged as we head toward Yosemite. This road winds through the California hills, providing some panoramic views of green hills and valleys. Approaching our destination, we find that the road follows a winding river with clear water, tumbling over and around rocks of many sizes. Mountains of trees and rocks rise on either side of us. I'm telling you, this is country!

Snow starts appearing farther back into the mountains. Waterfalls dot the mountainside. We are almost there.

We enjoy some hiking after we arrive in Yosemite Valley. We take the short trail to Lower Yosemite Falls and taste the water. It's cold and clear.

20

THE GRAND CANYON IN WINTER

DECEMBER 28

One good night's sleep and a hearty breakfast later, four of us tackle the mountain again. This time we want a better view of Upper Yosemite Falls. Glenn stays behind to visit the gift shop.

Our bus is scheduled to leave Yosemite Lodge at 10:00 a.m., so we want to be prompt in getting up the trail and back down. The trail is fairly easy to hike, though it rises a lot. Much of the trail has green foliage overhead. We are rewarded with a beautiful view of Yosemite Valley after arriving at a lookout point. Then we continue on.

On the last leg of the hike up the mountain, Myron and Freeman are held up. Freeman thinks he sees a bear. It ends up being only a rock or some inanimate object. Oh well, it provided some extra excitement, at least.

After getting a fairly decent view of the Upper Falls, we decide it's time to head back down. The trail we are on supposedly continues all the way up to the top of the falls. That one has "next time" written all over it.

After taking the bus back to Merced, we board a train bound for Bakersfield. An interesting thing occurs. The train is quite full, probably more so than any we've been on so far. We realize it might be difficult to find seats together for five of us, so we split up. I spot a pair of seats with no one in them, but according to the items on one of the seats, it appears one is taken and one is available. I make myself at home.

Soon though, two boys appear and inform me I am in their seats. My apologies.

I end up being thankful that I lost my seat.

I mosey up the aisle and find an empty seat next to a lady of sixty. She is reading a book entitled *The Shack*. Though I have not read the book, I am somewhat familiar with it and know it is a Christian story. When I comment on the book, it leads to quite a conversation.

She is a Christian lady named Mary, who lives in California. She shares some of her life story, how she grew up with an alcoholic father, accepted Christ at an early age, and with her husband, formerly ran a ministry smuggling Bibles into the Soviet Union. Mary seems to rejoice after learning that we, as Amish, also believe that Jesus Christ is the Son of God who came to earth to save us from our sins.

Before we part ways, we agree to pray for each other. She also asks me to pray for her daughters. Mary seems discouraged with the state of the world and says it is becoming more and more a "world without God." She thinks it would be "almost heaven" to live in a sheltered community like we do. Looking at it through her eyes, I think she's right. Funny how *she* made that plain to *me*.

DECEMBER 29

Today we hit the beach in Santa Barbara, California. It feels like the temperature is around seventy degrees and the sun is shining nicely.

As we are standing on the beach in the sun, wearing swimming trunks, Ivan muses that at home in northern Indiana, our loved ones are probably shoveling snow. A measure of delight is taken in this thought, as evidenced by Ivan's belly laugh.

Later we call the weather number and learn it is twenty-five degrees at home. Tee-hee.

DECEMBER 30

"Forty-five minutes 'til your stop. Forty-five minutes 'til your stop." It is five o'clock in the morning, and the conductor is waking us up.

Ivan is just a bit miffed. "Forty-five minutes! Couldn't he wake us up ten or fifteen minutes before it's time to get off?"

Poor Sweetness is being cheated out of his beauty sleep.

Our stop is Williams Junction, Arizona, which seems to be in the middle of nowhere. Thankfully, a bus is waiting there to take us to nearby Williams. At Williams, we can relax on luxurious leather sofas in front of a fireplace in the hotel while we wait until it's time to eat breakfast.

We enjoy a breakfast buffet at the nearby restaurant and watch the Wild West Show put on by the Grand Canyon Railway. Soon it's time to board.

This train, running from Williams to the Grand Canyon, is an older type of train. An entertainer is on board, and eventually he visits our car to sing a few songs. One melody is about getting married to a widow with six orphans, a great big ranch, and a ten-story home.

When we finally reach the Grand Canyon, snow is falling thickly.

After waiting impatiently for a bus, we decide to walk to our hotel, the Maswick Lodge. It is still snowing rather hard.

After thousands of miles, train trips, bus trips, taxi trips, and now walking, we finally stroll up to the rim of the Grand Canyon and see . . . not much. The snow is falling hard enough to limit visibility to a few hundred feet. With a sight as magnificent as the Grand Canyon, that type of visibility does not come close to doing justice.

We are disappointed and hope that the next morning will bring better visibility. It will have to be early, since we plan to leave the Grand Canyon at 10:15 a.m.

This night we have only one hotel room for five boys. Two beds and a cot already occupy the room. When five young men and all their baggage move in, it becomes quite crowded.

DECEMBER 31

We are up and at it early this final morning of the year. We want to see and hike the Grand Canyon before we leave.

The weather report says the temperature here is four degrees below zero. We, however, are from northern Indiana and are not deterred.

It is dark and cold as we walk to the rim. As the day breaks, we are rewarded. God has given us a beautiful, clear day. We enjoy some magnificent sunrise views of the Grand Canyon while hiking down Bright Angel Trail.

We don't see many other hikers at this hour. We gung ho Yankees are some of the few who are crazy enough to venture down the trail right now.

We time ourselves carefully, and after only forty-five minutes of descent, we turn around and hike for the top again. We meet some hikers now and reach the rim in time to watch the mule train begin its descent into the canyon.

We catch a shuttle to Flagstaff, Arizona. Once there, we have the afternoon to relax since our train doesn't leave until the next morning. I finish reading my book, *Lincoln the Unknown*, and do a bit of writing.

JANUARY 1

A gorgeous first day of the year, weather-wise. It is seven degrees above zero when we walk to the train station this morning to catch our 6:06 train. It is the Southwest Chief, bound for Chicago.

One of the intriguing aspects of traveling by train is the people you meet from all walks of life. We eat breakfast with a NASA engineer. She helps design the satellites that orbit the earth.

JANUARY 2

Some of my friends got to know a preacher from Spain, and as more people board the train, two teachers sit right in front of us. They are not traveling together, and it is just coincidence that they both sit close to us.

One is my age and a teacher's aide for first grade, and the other is a former high school English teacher, now a guidance counselor. The latter is a cousin of our local chiropractor, Norm Miller, in Middlebury. I extend my sympathies to her. (Only joking, Dr. Miller.) Small world. She is able to give me some enlightenment on my question of when to use *who* and *whom*.

Before arriving in Chicago, Ivan and I play a few Rook games with Henry Mullett and Daryl Mast. Daryl is the son of Norman, whose family is returning home to our area from a western trip.

Freeman and Myron, along with Norman Mast, teach an Air Force mechanic how to play our version of Rook.

Ivan and I have a nice conversation with a Chicagoan in the lounge car. She is a Christian, a Lutheran, and is excited about a possible job offer from a humanitarian outfit in Chicago that builds houses for the poverty-stricken.

We arrive in Chicago in cold temperatures.

There are some delays to our last train to Elkhart. Before too long though, we are on our way. It sure has been fun, yet I am glad to be going home. This trip has entertained, excited, and enlightened. And it's just so much the better that I get to go home to my friends, my parents, my pupils, my people. My very own "almost heaven."

21

THE CHILDREN OF ISRAEL
ENTER RURAL TOPEKA

IT IS MARCH 1. The car in which I am a passenger crunches into the snow-crusted driveway past the auction sign. Freeman S.'s son Vernon is having a farm sale today.

Vernon directs us to unload my sound system into the shop. Vernon has an unusually preoccupied air about him, though there is not a huge number of people around yet. I said not yet.

Vernon's son, my friend Calvin, takes me through the shop building, which is jammed with merchandise. He imparts instructions on how I should sell it and tells me not to dawdle while at it. He wants us finished by one o'clock this afternoon or one-thirty at the latest, which is when they want to sell their collection of Belgian draft horses, one of the big attractions today.

I locate some coffee and later a cinnamon roll. People are piling in. Vernon and Calvin want to counsel with the "help" (auctioneers, ringmen, and clerks) at 8:30 in the stately house on the northwest corner of the cluster of buildings here. That leaves some time to inspect the auction items. A tent stretches south from the house toward the barn and contains harnesses as well as some sporting goods. Nine loaded wagons rest beside it, containing a wide variety of merchandise. The field has rows of miscellaneous items, in addition to a few ranks of sleek farm equipment. Then there is the shop building where I'm to do the selling. It contains dozens of tables laden with household items as well as primitives and old and new toys. Several rows of furniture occupy the other third of the shop and await the gavel.

Freeman S., Vernon's father, is here, catching up with old pals and bursting out in a belly laugh now and then. It seems there is always a twinkle in his eye, though this must be a bittersweet day for him. He farmed here before Vernon did, and he is intimately familiar with some of the merchandise because he worked with it. Now the farm is being passed on to the next generation, Vernon's son Junior.

Did I mention people are coming? A week ago Vernon's neighbors chipped in with thirteen additional skid loaders to clear snow for parking space in the field. Two long cables are stretched. Each will accommodate a double column of horses and buggies. These fill up. The entire fenceline by the road fills with tied horses. Some of our people unhitch their steeds and tie them between the hitched horses at the cables, saving room. Vernon told me last week he is expecting to give out between four and five hundred buyer numbers today. I was a bit skeptical. That would be a huge auction.

The result? Six hundred and thirty-four people end up signing in to buy.

• • •

The crew gathers in Vernon and Marietta's kitchen at 8:30. Vernon gives us our assignments. My comrades in the loaded shop today are to be LaVern Miller, a young, married, auburn-bearded auctioneer from LaGrange; Dennis Helmuth, a fine ringman from Topeka; and Vernon Yoder of Gordyville fame and Allen Brenneman, both hailing from the Arthur, Illinois, area. These last three are experienced auction ringworkers, and I appreciate them many times before the day ends.

Many of us have worked together before, and there is some friendly trash talk going on. Vernon Miller again tells our shop crew that he wants us finished by one o'clock and not to mess around. I ask him what he wants me to do after we're finished at eleven o'clock. Vernon throws a golf ball at me.

We march outside to begin. A huge crowd of our fellow community members are blanketing the premises. Dean Yoder, an auctioneer from Illinois, begins the festivities on one of the wagons; he is soon followed by auctioneer Eli Miller Jr., on another wagon. Per instructions, we wait until 9:15 to begin in the shop, so I have a few minutes to listen to the smooth hums of Dean and Junior. Fun, fun.

When we do begin in the shop, we try to set a brisk pace. Yoder, Helmuth, and Brenneman know what they're doing, and there is little time wasted. A collection of Vernon's old wool hats kicks things off—seven count, at $17.50 each. A lot of merchandise quickly falls under LaVern's and my gavel, including glassware, Tupperware, puzzles, games, Coleman lanterns, and primitives. Vernon and Marietta's relatives help to keep the prices up by bidding on what they want. Calvin and his siblings get into a few bidding wars on nostalgic items. Calvin ends up buying a battered toy semi from his childhood for $75, and his sister, Edith, pays $500 for a fine old chest that has already been handed down for a few generations.

Despite our efforts, we see we're running behind schedule. I explain this to everyone and they help by bidding quickly. We careen through a selection of Calvin's new toys. They sell well and Calvin is left grinning. When the toys are over, we march through furniture. LaVern pronounces the last item in the shop sold at 1:24, and we begin to relax.

Junior is still selling farm equipment in the field east of the buildings. I join the mass of people there while the horse sale ring is being set up between the tent and the shop. Horse enthusiasts find seats and continue socializing while they wait for that segment to begin.

In the field Junior sells the feed grinder for $7,000 and the old Minneapolis Moline tractor on hard rubber wheels for three grand. After he drops the hammer on the JCB skid loader, this segment is done and everyone is ready for the horse ring. We see in the distance the mass of people already seated around the horse ring. We who were in the field must look like the children of Israel, moving in to join them.

Dean Yoder assumes the auctioneer's microphone, and his father, the Illinois Vernon, assumes the commentator's to sell the brawny Belgian horses to the standing-room-only crowd. Vernon Miller's big blonde stallion goes first, ending up with a ticket to Wisconsin for $6,300. After that, many of the mares come through the ring hooked in teams. There is a demand for these field-ready mares, and they sell mostly between $2,500 and $3,500. One fancy young filly sells for $4,000.

We wrap up the day with some lighter buggy horse stock. When Dean has dropped the gavel on the last steed, Vernon Miller finally takes the microphone. He thanks everyone for their attendance and offers to pay for lunch for all of us who helped with the auction.

Some people make for the office to pay for their purchases. Some, like me, trot to the food stand that is set up in a shop building. After we have our food, we sit at the tables made from church benches put together. Vernon eats and decompresses along with us as we discuss the day's happenings. We mull over why some items sold much higher than we expected and why others seemed cheap. The consensus is that Vernon had a wildly successful sale. Referring to the huge crowd of people, I tell Vernon, "You must have a lot of friends." Vernon shrugs it off.

Vernon does have a lot of friends. He also knows that the biggest factor was the community that lives around here. The community helped prepare for the sale, bid, bought, sold food, and did whatever it took. The community made it happen.

PART III

Spring

22

SCHOOL VISITATION

I HATE TO break it to you," teacher Mike Lambright, tongue-in-cheek, tells his Cloverleaf pupils, "but I guess we'll go play a game of softball."

A softball game should be a thrilling end to our delightful day of visiting schools so far. Our school's sixth, seventh, and eighth graders, as well as a few parents and we teachers, have visited eight schools and the Subway in Topeka already today.

We have been welcomed warmly, like at Spring Valley the first thing this morning. Teachers Johnny Lambright and Barb Miller made us feel at home even though we showed up before any of their students did. The praise songs we sang at Spring Valley during devotions were a fitting way to commence the day.

We have been entertained and educated, like at Northside. This second school we visited sang the "President Song" three times through before coming to an abrupt stop. I hadn't realized Grover Cleveland served two separate terms. Now I know.

We have seen education in action, like at Little Acorn. Arithmetic and reading classes were held as we observed.

We have been awed by state-of-the-art facilities, like at Buck Creek in LaGrange. What would we do with *all* that room?

Rosetta Eicher and her co-teacher hold classes in a spacious, nearly new building.

We have been humbled and impressed by children's sportsmanship, like at Countryside. Edna Yoder and Leona Mast's crew simply does an exceptional job of encouraging everyone, be it teammate or opponent. They do an exceptional job of hitting softballs too, if the final score was any indicator.

We have had our rumbling stomachs satisfied, like at the little Subway in Topeka. There were a few tables there but not enough for our crew of fourteen, so some of us stood to eat our sandwiches.

We have been soundly trounced at a game of softball, like at Whispering Wind. My friend Calvin welcomed us warmly, and then he and his students socked it to us fair and square on the diamond. My chance to get a lick in came when Calvin asked me to tell his school a story. I told everyone about the time we tricked Calvin and took him to Kentucky instead of Pennsylvania as he had been planning. (We actually made it to Kentucky in broad daylight before he noticed something was amiss.)

We have been encouraged, like at Eden Meadow. They sang the song "*Gott Isz Grosz*" in our native Pennsylvania German, which reminded us that no matter how tough the circumstances, God is, indeed, great.

We have even done some acting, like at Clay Ridge. Steve Mast's wife, Ida, evidently found out we were planning to visit her children's school. She told teachers Joella Knepp, Alice Bontrager, and Martha Miller in no uncertain terms that they were to make us perform for them when we came. This they did. And we tried to oblige. Co-teacher Delmar and I performed a skit after we enjoyed watching Joella's German spelling class.

To be fair, when Clay Ridge visited us last week, we put them on the spot and had them perform a play for us. Ida starred in the role of Amelia Bedelia, which may explain her desire for reciprocation.

Now here we are at Cloverleaf, ready to attempt to win at least one ball game today. Mike and Merlin have a chipper group of students, and we all move out to the ball diamond. Mike himself is fighting a lingering back injury and doesn't play. His presence is still felt as he manages his squad skillfully and fills the role of umpire behind the plate.

Cloverleaf's team is long on girls and short on boys. What they do not lack is athletic ability and intelligence. We hit well and soon have a commanding lead, but Cloverleaf claws back into it and, in fact, loads the bases with two outs in the bottom of the last inning. We are clinging to our suddenly tiny-looking three-run lead. Teacher Merlin is up to bat, but he mercifully pops to shortstop Delmar and we escape with a win.

These games, either wins or losses, soon will be merely grains in the sand of time. A day like this, though, spent with people you love and doing something this memorable, is a precious pearl to capture and savor.

23

SIGN YOUR NOTES, SMARTY!

THE NOTE WAS written in block letters, lying innocently on my desk at school. "ATTENTION!" it demanded in big red caps on the outside.

Inside, the text was again in block letters (the better to remain anonymous, my dear). "LAST WEEK IN OUR SPELLING WORDS," it began, "WE HAD THE WORD 'SECRETIVE.' YOU PRO-NOUNCED IT 'SÉE-KRUT-IV.' THE CORRECT PRONUNCIATION IS 'SI-KRÉET-IV.'"

Indeed. (Later, when I checked more advanced dictionar-ies, I discovered that I had been, in fact, correct. But for the moment, we roll with it.)

The note, of course, was unsigned—rather like something out of an Encyclopedia Brown mystery story. There was no need to put a quarter on the gas can, though. I planned to fig-ure it out myself.

Being corrected did not bother me very long. Much better to swallow correction once and be forever wiser than to appear ignorant every time you say the word and have no one brave enough to tell you that you mispronounced it.

Actually, I'm quite fond of the idea of students digging deeper than their teacher digs and finding out for themselves the truth of the matter. I think it's a healthy culture—within reason.

I remember friend Paul Devon Hochstetler telling how his teacher, Wendell Bailey, would slip a quarter onto pupils' desks if they caught him making a mistake. That, my friends, is the atmosphere I want.

It was the manner of correction that puzzled me a bit. Why did she—yeah, I'm fairly certain it was a *she*—employ all the cloak-and-dagger stuff? I mean, the thing looked like a ransom note.

First, I wanted to determine for certain who the protagonist was. Here comes my Sherlock Holmes hat. Without much thought, I narrowed it down to two eighth-grade ladies. When you teach a group of students for three-plus years, you get a feel for personalities and tendencies. Quite elementary, Watson.

In addition, I had seen one of these fine scholars hanging around the classroom after the others were gone. She was number one on the list.

Of course, I could simply have asked the class as a whole who wrote the note and she probably would have admitted it. This is an honest bunch. But I'd prefer to have a bit more fun with it.

Next day, recess. A spirited game of darebase was going on. I managed to sneak around our eminent eighth grader's base and capture her teammate. Trooping past their base back to my own, I mentioned that I had been secretive in getting around them. I carefully watched this fourteen-year-old lady's face as I said it.

It was her. Sure enough. I feel like I could work for Scotland Yard. Now to communicate my point that she need not be, well, secretive about correcting me. Please enjoy my humble poetry. It describes what happened next.

This eighth-grade lady, she's so keen
A pronunciation queen.
Her teacher slipped, her ears were upped.
Secretive was the word he'd flubbed.

A note was writ, dropped on his desk,
Describing how he'd failed the test.
A name? She wrote none on the note.
"Don't want to seem *too* smart," she quotes.

Her teacher read, then had to smile,
Reached into his memory file.
He knows who 'twas, no need to fuss
E'en though it was anonymous.

He thought a bit, then applied the squeeze.
"Come up here to my desk, please.
Thanks, thanks to you, I'm up to par.
Your reward? Enjoy this candy bar.

"Like you, I am at school to learn.
And with this thought, let us adjourn.
I stand corrected, hale and hearty.
Now sign your notes, you little smarty!"

24

WISECRACK WANDA'S SLUMP

WISECRACK WANDA is in a slump. Her customary scream-ing line drives have given way to weak foul balls and strikeouts. Wanda's usual happy chatter while perched on first or second base has changed to an irate grumbling as she makes her way back to the bench after striking out. Wanda is perplexed and frustrated. After all, she's in the eighth grade. She should have this figured out by now.

Now the pressure level rises. Tumbling Creek School comes strolling across the schoolyard. They are on their round of school visiting and have happened to arrive here at Sunrise Valley School at recess time. This provides an excel-lent opportunity for a friendly ball game—Tumbling Creek versus Sunrise Valley.

The excitement level rises on the playground as positions are quickly decided. The home team, Sunrise Valley, soon takes the field and Tumbling Creek sends up their first batters. Through all the excitement, Wisecrack Wanda feels an apprehension growing in her stomach. These spring ball games between schools are much anticipated, and this should be one of the highlights of her eighth-grade year. With this slump though,

Wanda feels as likely to strike out as get a solid hit should she happen to bat in a clutch situation.

A three-inning game is decided upon, to allow Tumbling Creek to stay on their school-visiting schedule and to allow Sunrise Valley sufficient time to do their schoolwork after the ball game.

Tumbling Creek quickly gets on the board by scoring a few runs in the top of the first inning. They add a few more in the second and really pour it on in their half of the third, making the score 9–1 in Tumbling Creek's favor. Further damage is averted by Wisecrack Wanda's classmate Towering Tommy Miller, who angles over from his position at first base to catch a high foul ball hit by a Tumbling Creek parent, also joining in the ball game.

We at Sunrise Valley scratched out our lone run in the bottom of the second, when Chipper Chester turned on the jets and steamed from first to home on a blooping single by a sixth-grade girl.

But now, in the bottom of the third and last inning, we find ourselves down eight runs. The outlook isn't brilliant. Further darkening any hopes of a late rally, sixth grader Hustling Harriet lines out gently while leading off the bottom of the third.

After that, however, business begins to pick up. Another sixth-grade girl, not known for her heavy hitting, sneaks a grounder past the shortstop to earn a spot on first base.

The next hitter happens to be me. I knock one into the outfield that slips under the glove of Tumbling Creek's center fielder. When the ball is retrieved and the throw comes in, I am puffing from third base to home. Tumbling Creek's shortstop fires a strike to the catcher, who applies the tag just as I step onto home plate. The umpire, another Tumbling Creek parent, shows excellent sportsmanship and pronounces me safe.

The gap is now six and Sunrise Valley is loosening up. The bench begins to holler and cheer.

A series of well-placed grounders and solid base hits scores a few more runs, ratchets the intensity up, and loads the bases with two outs. Now the score stands 9–5, and the tying run comes up to bat in the form of none other than Wisecrack Wanda.

This is exactly the type of situation Wanda normally would have relished. Today, though, she dreads it. She has not smacked a solid hit in what seems like ages. To her, it seems a distinct probability that she will let her team down.

With typical abruptness, she chides herself as she steps to the plate. "C'mon Wanda! Keep on swinging. Hit the ball. Hit it hard. You've done it before."

After letting only one pitch go past for a ball, Wanda finds one she likes. Showing not a trace of timidity, Wisecrack Wanda hacks at the ball. Her slender frame uncoils like a spring as she swings the bat with all her might. This time she hits it. She hits it well.

A fly ball rises toward left-center field. Tumbling Creek's outfielder in that position, an eighth-grade girl who is a capable athlete herself, makes haste in retreating. Sunrise Valley's bench anticipates an extra-base hit and begins to erupt. This could break the game wide open.

Running backward and reaching up, though, the lass makes the catch. The comeback is not to be.

Recess is over now, and after high fives, everyone makes their way to the schoolhouse. After a brief visit, Tumbling Creek is on its way again, with a victory.

Wisecrack Wanda and her mates at Sunrise Valley have something they will learn to appreciate more as the years go by, though. They have memories. Memories of excellent sportsmanship, of a team pulling together, and of keeping on swinging, no matter what.

25

MUDVILLE MADNESS

AMERICA LOVES an underdog. This time, though, the underdog has a problem. The problem's name is LaVern Lehman. His moonshots are legendary, and his muscular two-hundred-and-eighty pounds stands at the plate waving the bat with an ease born of formidable strength.

It is the year-end ball game at the school picnic. The "game of games" is underway: the fathers of the school, ten in all, versus eleven elementary students and us two teachers.

Today began a bit ominously, with heavy rain in the morning. The sun did shine earlier this afternoon, but not enough to dry out the ball diamond. By this evening, it is a muddy, slippery, sodden mess. The soggy conditions are not enough, though, to stop this highly anticipated matchup.

The evening's program has been completed, and the eighth graders graduated with due ceremony. The picnic and bystanders are spread out behind home plate. Now the ball game is on.

We take the field first. These youngsters are as charged as thoroughbreds behind the starting gate. I daresay we teachers are a bit fired up, too.

We shut out the men in the top of the first—going through only four batters to do it.

My competitive juices overflow in our half of the first inning, as I am overly aggressive on the base paths. I am caught and tagged out between second and third. In the process, I slip on the spongy grass and splash to the ground, thereby soaking my bottom side. The seventh-grade base runner ahead of me scampers home to score, though, and we lead by one. All is not in vain.

The men quickly jump into the lead, though, with two runs in the top of the second, and the seesaw battle is on. Back and forth through the game we go, becoming muddier by sudden spurts, neither team able to obtain a big lead over the other.

The scholars are playing solid defense in spite of the soggy conditions, and we are stringing together enough rallies on offense to poke our noses into the lead occasionally.

In one highlight, my light-hitting co-teacher smacks one into left field. Hard. The ball sails over the trampoline-sized puddle beside the foul line and over speedy left fielder Menno Lehman's head. Then, from the gladdened multitude, there rises a joyous yell. Our lady teacher has an extra-base hit. The next time she comes up to bat, Menno makes a great show of retreating farther into the outfield.

We approach the end. Into the seventh and last inning we go. A two-run lead is our scanty cushion.

Rain clouds are threatening again in the west, and the men, batting in the top of the seventh, soon are too. These muscle-bound ballplayers score a run, further trimming our slim margin to the slimmest possible. Worse yet, they load the bases with two outs, ready to take a solid lead.

And here comes the next batter, now approaching the plate, now dropping his extra bat and waving the remaining one like a toothpick in his meaty hands: "Mighty Casey" himself. LaVern Lehman is up to bat.

A collective shudder runs through the defense. This man is famous locally for his prodigious drives. Softballs are known to rocket off his bat and become tiny in the distance.

LaVern Lehman the man is friendly and easy to get along with. LaVern Lehman the hitter is to be feared.

As the pitcher, my job is to keep him off balance. LaVern is too experienced a ballplayer to be easily tricked, though, and he knows I can ill afford to walk him and force home the tying run. I have to pitch to him.

Eventually, I do. LaVern selects one he likes and swings with that fluid, powerful stroke. He smashes it high and deep into left-center field.

It is not, however, one of LaVern's best shots. He didn't get it all.

The outfield was playing deep, and the seventh grader in left-center has time to move under it and make the catch. Mighty Casey has flown out.

The outfielder squeezes the ball for a moment and then flings it into the air in jubilation. Happy cries erupt from every corner of the field, and the scholars have difficulty suppressing the wide grins on their faces as we high-five the men. We don't always win—and we don't have to—but this one is sweet.

There is great joy in Mudville.

26

THE SHELLACKING

BRADLEY MILLER drags the three-foot section of the ladder into the outfield and, with exaggerated deliberation, props it against the fence in the deepest part of center field. "There you go, guys!" he crows to his opponents. "Don't ever say I'm not a nice guy. I put up a ladder to make it easier for you fellows to get over the fence to chase the balls we hit."

His cousins on the other team fire back quick retorts. Their flaming determination to beat him is manifested in a slow shaking of their heads as they continue to toss softballs back and forth, limbering up.

Bragging Brad is at it again. He is known among all his friends and relatives as a youngster who makes great boasts about his abilities and intentions—and even backs up a few of them.

This vocal lad is a well-built, stocky, black-haired twenty-two-year-old of average height and average athletic ability, but tremendous enthusiasm. His bubbling energy level, when not applied to some specific task, often manifests itself in friendly bantering. Brad subconsciously knows that there is one likely way you can kindle a friendly argument—by boasting about your intentions. So if Brad needs an outlet, he often finds it by stating and restating his grand intentions, firing back at the contradictions of his opponents. Bragging Brad really doesn't consider himself better; he just enjoys the thrill of the argument.

Today he finds dry tinder for his sparks. Bragging Brad's opponents fling back stinging remarks and put more go in their throw and spring in their swing as they warm up.

• • •

The Miller Boys, as Bradley and his fellow eastern cousins are called, are visiting their western cousins in Montana. Competitiveness is the common denominator in this extended family, regardless which side of the Mississippi they hail from. A "West versus East" ball game is suggested and instantly accepted with much enthusiasm. The trash talk begins, with Bradley leading the way.

"I'm going into business," one declares. "I'll set up an ibuprofen stand. These grandpappies from the West will be begging for it."

"Not so fast!" retorts a western opponent. "You eastern pups aren't used to this altitude. I'd put up an oxygen tank at second base for you—if I thought you'd ever get that far."

"C'mon, you chaps!" Bragging Brad urges. "Let's get started. I can't wait to see the back end of these western wimps as they chase the balls we Beasts from the East hit."

And so the Beasts from the East face off against the Best of the West. They truly do love each other, and if any one of them finds himself in a tight spot, he can expect help coming from sea to shining sea. Now, though, they really, really want to win this game. The intensity is palpable.

The East's leadoff batter rips a screamer down the left field line, thirty feet left of fair territory.

"Foul!" cries the umpire.

"Foul?" howls Uncle Calvin on the sidelines. "If that one's foul, they're all foul."

These boys' competitiveness was not stolen. Indeed, the preceding generation itself exhibits plenty of fire.

• • •

It soon becomes apparent that the West will carry the day. Time after time, their muscular hitters chase Bragging Brad over his ladder by clobbering balls far beyond his position in center field. Meanwhile, the East is having a poor hitting day, and they hit very few balls that even approach the fence.

The shellacking continues. One westerner, after crossing home plate after his home run, turns around to watch cousin Brad climb back over the ladder into the field of play. "Thanks for putting up that ladder for us, Brad," he calls, grinning broadly. "You really are a considerate chap."

"Hush," Brad says. He is much too winded to add to it.

• • •

The West ends up winning by a score of 24–3. The East promptly returns the favor the next evening on the volleyball court. The debate about who the best athletes are continues, as such debates do. No one will ever win these arguments, but they will certainly enjoy trying.

27

MURDER MOUNTAIN

THE RECORD FOR climbing Murder Mountain is three and a half hours. Bragging Bradley Miller is unimpressed.

The Ohio native stands outside his cousin's Montana home, gazing up at the range of mountains to the east. "You mean that little molehill? We'll do it in two and a half—if we take it easy."

The band of cousins around him, some from Montana, some from Ohio, are not so sure. "It's farther than you think, Brad," one cautions. "And don't forget the air gets thinner as we go up, plus we'll all be wearing packs. This is no walk in the park."

Bragging Brad loves an argument and he is undeterred.

"Don't worry," Bradley says, in a sarcastically soft tone. "If you fellows get too tired, I'll wear your pack as well as mine. Maybe I'll even take Grandpa's wheelchair along, so I can push you over the rough places."

When Bradley's boundless energy is not bent to a specific task, it often bursts out in spirited bantering. Over the years he has honed his arguing skills to an art, and he knows the easiest way to get a lively verbal contest started is by making terrific boasts. Immediately his almost equally competitive comrades will begin disputing his abilities, and the brouhaha is on— which is exactly what he wants.

• • •

The morning of the hike dawns clear and unseasonably warm. The well-prepared hikers put a few more Gatorade beverages in the packs.

One lad disappears for several minutes and returns with a sly grin on his face, lugging a soccer-ball-sized rock that has been recruited from a nearby flower bed. He glances around and whispers conspiratorially, "Why don't we put this rock in Brad's pack and see if he still thinks he can hike the mountain in two and a half hours?" The cumbersome rock is placed at the bottom of a pack filled with Gatorade. The boys make sure the rock is completely covered with bottles.

Then along comes Bragging Brad himself, fairly bouncing with excitement and raring to conquer Murder Mountain. Quickly putting an innocent expression on his face, one young man hands Brad the inconspicuous pack containing the drinks.

"Here's a nice, light one for you to carry," he says graciously. "We sure don't want to have to push you along in the wheelchair." Brad just smiles in a superior sort of way and lets the comment pass. He grabs the pack that his friend hands to him and slings it onto his back. The others watch out of the corners of their eyes and make a gallant effort not to laugh as he staggers backward several steps. His eyes bug out slightly.

"Something the matter?" one boy asks, a concerned look on his face.

"Of course not!" Brad snaps, forcing a smile.

The boys begin the trek up Murder Mountain. To his credit, Brad utters no word of complaint but trudges steadily on, though he is sweating profusely.

Whenever someone feels in need of a drink, they just reach into the pack on Brad's back and withdraw a bottle of Gatorade. The boys soon realize, however, that by doing so they are making his load lighter. So they acquire several fist-sized stones, and every drink that they take out of Brad's pack is replaced with a small rock.

"Is your load getting lighter now that we're drinking the Gatorade?" one boy inquires.

"Actually," Brad huffs, "I can't really say that it is."

The farther they hike, the more poor Brad's shoulders slump under the strain. His face is grim and his breathing labored. Finally, he can stand it no more. He sprawls onto the nearest rock and demands a break.

"A break!" one young man protests. "We can't make it to the top in two and a half hours if we're taking breaks all the time!" Brad ignores him and opens his pack for a drink. He freezes at the unexpected sight of a dozen fist-sized stones sitting on top of the Gatorade. He glances at his comrades, who have suddenly discovered urgent business elsewhere. The pranksters, however, are soon ducking for cover as the rocks rain down upon them from the hand of Bragging Bradley. He is *not* amused.

Feeling that it would be best to confess everything right away, one of his comrades mercifully tells Brad he may want to check the bottom of his pack, too, before he continues. The soccer ball-sized rock is soon produced. Brad snatches up his pack, now much lighter, and stalks off, his snickering companions not far behind.

They safely complete the hike, and it is not until several months later that Bragging Bradley can see any humor in the joke.

One of the boys, seeing the souvenir quality of the notorious rock, lugs it back down the mountain. A few years later, on Bradley's wedding day, all the jokesters sign it and give it to him as a present.

While opening gifts from their guests after the wedding feast, Bradley's new bride discovers the infamous stone, about which she knows nothing. A small smile begins to tug at Brad's mouth. "Well, you see, honey," he says, putting his hand on her shoulder, "we went on a hiking trip once, and the other Miller boys were afraid they wouldn't be able to keep up . . ."

28

MY FRIEND, THE LEGEND

THE VALLEY LIES resplendent below us. Farmers' green fields and winding roads complement the dark green of tree lines, presenting a spectacle quite pleasing to the eye. The gorgeous view amply compensates for the rough horseback ride up here and the abuse we suffered at the hands of our female companions ere we ever mounted one steed.

Fellow travelers Amzie Lehman, Steven Miller, Calvin Miller, Esther Lehman, and my sister Emily accompanied me on a train trip to Pennsylvania this weekend. We arrived in Lancaster and were greeted there by our friend and host Eli Stolzfus.

After enjoying a weekend of socializing with our Pennsylvania friends, we loaded into a van along with ten Pennsylvania ladies and gentlemen and headed westward toward the Nittany Valley of Pennsylvania. There we planned to have a trail ride.

Perhaps the whole battle started when one of the boys snitched Sadie Mae's wallet at the restaurant at breakfast, or perhaps it started when three pieces of boys' headwear were snatched by the girls and doused with ladies' perfume. I would, of course, favor the latter as the cause of it all, but as in the case of the "shot heard round the world," no one knows who started it, but it certainly sparked quite a ruckus.

The biggest tactical mistake the boys' army made was allowing the girls to occupy the two rear seats of our fourteen-passenger van when we left the restaurant. If there is mischief to be done, those in the rear have a distinct advantage. In a related misfortune, my sister, Emily, ended up in the position directly behind mine.

As many of you brothers know from experience, birds fly, fish swim, horses kick, dogs chase cats, and sisters pull their brothers' hair when they're aggravated. Evidently, it's natural. After a few of those tear-jerking yanks, I was nearly ready to go storming over the seat back and occupy my sister's seat in order to restore order.

As painful as these episodes were, the misuse of my hat was possibly worse. I mean, this cowboy is not that rugged of a man, but to have my hat sprayed, doused, and soaked in ladies' perfume is just a bit much. I want to wear that derby to horse sales, after all.

Despite the ongoing abuse, I endured without making an attempt to displace the troublemakers. When, however, I heard a distracting hiss and felt perfume hitting the back of my head, that was enough.

Like George Pickett and his rebels, I went charging up Cemetery Ridge—in this case, the seatback behind me. And like the unfortunate Pickett, I was repelled by a show of strength from the entrenched position. I withdrew, stewing, to lick my wounds.

At the first rest stop, compadres Calvin and Sam Schmucker joined me in snatching the briefly unoccupied rear seat of the van. Now we had the troublemakers surrounded, and things proceeded much more peacefully thenceforth. Strategy is important in these matters.

• • •

We arrived around midday in Nittany Valley, at the farm Eli owns and rents to his sister's family. Those who have done this before point out the bald spot at the crest of the mountain, way over there, where we want to camp tonight.

We pick out horses. I select a leggy chestnut with three white socks, a decent neck, and a nice, straight head. I later find out he is a Dutch Harness cross. An unusual saddle horse, perhaps, but he ends up performing quite well. I name him Torpedo. Torp for short.

When we finally have all sixteen horses tacked up, we point our horses' noses toward the mountain to the south of us. We ride for high ground.

• • •

"I came here to London to become a legend and I am a legend. . . . I've done all I want to do. I've got no more goals."

Usain Bolt had this to say after he won a few more gold medals at the Olympics. We found his quote in the newspaper I purchased before boarding the train in Pittsburgh to continue our journey to Lancaster, Pennsylvania.

Our group of six Hoosiers chews on this unusual quote for a bit. It sounds like something companion Calvin Miller would say in jest. I assume Mr. Bolt was serious.

The trail slopes upward to the base of the mountain, where we begin to climb in earnest. It is a beautiful day and a nice, wooded trail for a ride. It switches back and forth, climbing up the mountain.

When we reach the top, we ride eastward along the crest. Torpedo, the Dutch cross horse I'm riding, is doing well. Sam

Schmucker's Appaloosa is not. She balks sometimes at following the others, kicks a few times, and generally exhibits a sour
attitude. Calvin says she ought to be run over. Calvin is not
afraid of expressing his opinion. Many of us agree with him,
though, by the time this trip is over.

We stop at an opening along the crest where power lines
come through. Here we enjoy a view of the valley we left a few
hours ago. Those with experience say the view is better yet at
our destination to the northeast.

The trail winds east and north down this mountain and up
another one. Eventually, we spot the trailer loaded with our
camping supplies that someone trucked up here for us. Yes, we
cheated.

We do still have a steep, quarter-mile, winding trail to the
campsite that no truck and trailer will climb. But, oh, the view
when we get there.

The campsite is at a lookout point bare of trees on the crest
of the mountain. The ground drops away, steep and rocky, in
front of us. Far below us, the valley spreads out to the west. We
can see farms scattered out and the curving, silver road con-
necting them. The dark green of tree lines adds trim to the pat-
tern. It is gorgeous handiwork of God.

Now begins the chore of hauling our camping gear up the
mountain from the trailer to the campsite. Up and down the
trail we go, many of us hauling the gear on our horses until
we are sufficiently equipped—we think—at the top of the
mountain.

The horses' "stable" is between the trailer and our campsite. We scatter our steeds out, tying them to trees, giving them
water as well as hay and grain. They've earned it.

Somehow, the Appaloosa ends up tied right beside the trail where she manages to sneak in a kick or two at the horses going past. Where is a concrete truck when you need one?

Those who knew about the almost sheer drop-off into the valley away from our perch on the mountaintop have come prepared. They brought dozens of golf balls, along with a few clubs.

A well-hit ball is a sight to behold as it soars out over the valley before dropping into Iowa somewhere. We content ourselves for a bit by just watching the balls. Soon though, as boys will, we turn it into a competition and begin timing the flight of our drives.

Calvin soon owns the lead with a time of 10.7 seconds. We call it a world record. It is, as far as we know.

Soon after taking the lead, Calvin retires to play a card game while others continue launching golf balls into the atmosphere, challenging him. When asked why he doesn't attempt to improve his time, Calvin replies, in true Calvin fashion, "I came here to become a legend. Now I am a legend. I have no more goals."

29

THE BRICK LANDED IN PENNSYLVANIA

AMZIE LEHMAN has heard the conclusion of the brick story. He is not amused.

To be fair, the story does require a fairly versatile sense of humor, and to Amzie's credit, he laughs long and hard later—when he is the one telling the joke.

To recap, we are camping on the crest of a mountain overlooking the Nittany Valley with a group of Pennsylvania and Indiana friends.

The brick joke ideally includes two storytellers. The first will tell what seems like a lame joke about a pyramid builder who lofts his last brick into the sky because he's not allowed to take it back to the ground with him. This story usually falls pretty flat, and the teller looks like a chump.

Then, sometime later, maybe even the next day, another aspiring comedian will tell the story of a woman who lunges partway out of an airplane window to save a dog. When she pulls Fido back into the plane by the hind leg, what do you suppose he has in his mouth? The answer is, of course, the brick that the pyramid builder chucked straight into the air.

Amzie fails to see humor immediately. "You're not even allowed to open airplane windows," he protests. We remind him not to overthink it. Amzie has that tendency occasionally.

Days later, Amzie shares the joke with others, telling it with gusto. There is a lot to be said for someone with the ability to change his mind.

• • •

Eventually talk subsides, and we bed down for the night. I arrange my borrowed sleeping bag on the rocky ground as best I can and turn in.

Partway through the night we are awakened by raindrops on our faces. Ugh. I roll over and go back to sleep. Usually I'm not too ambitious at three-thirty in the morning.

Someone, though, is sufficiently concerned about our welfare to get out of a warm sleeping bag in these wee hours. Eli and Steven hike the quarter mile down to fetch the tarp and tents and then back up the steep mountainside. They set those up and I manage to find sufficient energy to drag my now damp sleeping bag into a tent where I enjoy another three hours of blissful sleep. Thanks, gents.

If you think by now that I'm not much of an outdoorsman, you are one hundred percent correct.

We finally get up, enjoy a leisurely breakfast, and begin the chore of carrying all our gear back down the mountain to the trailer. Before we leave though, some of the boys amuse themselves a bit with Sadie Mae's chair.

Sadie Mae is a charter member of a gang of girls that has been harassing us gentlemen this whole trip. Maybe the boys are trying to return the favor by messing with Sadie Mae's camping chair, or perhaps they're just amusing themselves. Either way, the chair keeps being moved farther down the steep bank of rocks bordering the campsite.

Sadie Mae stands at the edge, stick in hand, alternating between dire threats and humble pleas for someone to retrieve her chair. She uses threats the most, even if she looks like such a sweet girl.

Finally Amzie, like the gentleman he is, agrees to fetch it for her. Things are not always what they seem, though, and Amzie "trips" just as he reaches the top. The chair bounces down the mountainside and comes to rest at a much greater distance than before.

Amzie protests that he didn't intend for the chair to go that far. He can't help but laugh, though, at the crazy way the chair bounced over the rocks.

Levi Zook finally puts an end to the suspense by climbing down over the boulders and returning with the brick in his mouth. He gives the chair to its rightful owner without incident and eventually we are back on the trail.

30

GOD'S QUILT

THE SUN IS SINKING. I glance out the corner window in Vernon's shop, remembering the auction we held here just a few months ago. Then the visitation line moves. My gaze moves the other direction and downward, onto the old familiar face lying in the casket. Freeman S. has passed on.

I look my last. Of course, we'll hardly remember Freeman's face like this. Rather, the perpetually grinning, sparkly-eyed, belly-laughing Freeman S. is the one who will be lodged in our memory.

The line shuffles forward, shaking hands and murmuring a few words with Freeman's close relatives who are seated facing each other over a narrow aisle. And then, right behind the family, visible without being conspicuous, is the community.

This community is the one that turned out in huge numbers in March when Vernon had his farm auction. Now it is twelve weeks later and Vernon is burying his father. The community is here again.

When I read the obituary today, I was surprised to see how small Freeman's family is. He had two daughters and two sons—small by our standards. Usually it is large families that lend themselves to large auctions and large weddings, church services, baptisms, and funerals. Freeman didn't have many children. But there is support—all over the place.

There is LeRoy with his wife, Ida Mae. He lives across the fields, owns a woodworking business, and loves playing Rook. His daughters are students of Freeman's grandson, my friend Calvin. There are Elmer and Alice from a few miles up the road in Honeyville. They work at the same local sale barn where Freeman worked. Over yonder stand Tim and Violet. They live in the same Michigan community as Freeman's daughter Polly.

We've heard people say, "We don't fully realize what we have here in this community until something tragic happens to our family." Freeman died yesterday morning. Help poured in from neighbors and friends, who abandoned their plans for Saturday and came to make preparations for a funeral. I wasn't there, but Calvin tells me the barn was cleaned, floors were swept, things were moved, the shop was washed, and a tent was put up. I've seen it in our neighborhood, too.

On Monday night three inches of rain fell at Vernon's farm, where the funeral was to be held on Tuesday. Rain flooded the buggy parking area, ran through the toolshed where people were to be seated, and pooled in the barn. The neighbors anticipated this, and by 5:30 in the morning, people were pouring into the driveway. The mess was cleaned up without the family having to lift a finger.

A few years ago when an accident on the toll road claimed the lives of a few men in the same church, it was almost more than one district could handle. So the surrounding districts pitched in and picked up the slack—warmly, quickly, and compassionately.

We hope and we pray and we are thankful that this is how God intended it to be. Like a living patchwork quilt, each individual is connected to the pieces around him. Those pieces are connected to another ring beyond the first. When one piece, one soul, rejoices, the entire quilt rejoices. When one person suffers, the whole quilt suffers, and each piece reaches out toward the sufferer, doing what it can to ease the pain, to smooth the path.

Of course, we notice and appreciate the community at times of rejoicing, like at baptisms and weddings, or at business events, like auctions. But it is when we suffer a loss, when our hearts are left grasping for answers, that we feel Christ's church most acutely. It is there. It soothes. And it carries us through.

As any quilter will tell you, a quilt is only separate, flimsy pieces of fabric without thread and without a backing. The backing supporting us all is Jesus Christ. The thread holding us all together is love. And even that thread, that love, is God.

After all, God is love. And the community is simply an extension of Him.

PART IV

Summer

31

THE BEST WEST QUEST

AS I REMEMBER IT, the first shots were fired while we boys walked peaceably to McDonald's. When we had finished our breakfast and returned to the train station, my comfy neck pillow was completely wrapped in very unmanly hot pink duct tape.

So much for a nice, peaceful vacation. Apparently the girls want war.

In numbers, our group is evenly balanced with four ladies and four gentlemen. The girls consist of my sister Emily, Esther Lehman, her cousin Neomah Lehman, and Mary Eash. Mike Lambright, Steven Miller, and Calvin Miller join me in trying to keep the girls in order.

In applying sheer wit and audacity, though, we guys are already behind. The luminescent tape on my pillow is sufficient evidence of that. Very well, these two-and-a-half weeks of traveling should provide some opportunity to play offense. Lord willing, we plan to experience Ouray, Colorado; San Francisco, California; Modesto, California; Yosemite National Park; and St. Ignatius, Montana.

The driver has picked up all of us except Calvin, who plans to join us in Chicago this afternoon. We get off the van at the Amtrak station in Elkhart.

While we wait for our train, we three gentlemen use our extra time to walk to McDonald's for a bite to eat. Returning to the station, we make a grand entrance by racing through the parking lot and sprinting up to the crowded station like some crazy country bumpkins. It's only the first of many times on this trip that those around us will have cause to think us dim, ignorant, backward, or just plain loco. We rather enjoy it that way.

I remove the bright pink tape from my pillow, fearing it will detract from the comfort the pillow usually brings me. I tie the used tape around Calvin's unattended bag—adding a touch of the feminine.

There are many others waiting to board the train on this Saturday, June 29. When we finally board, the train is temporarily short on seats and we sit in the lounge car at the tables.

We take to it like a rabbit to a carrot patch. Quickly we get out the games. Settlers of Catan comes out early here, and it will come out often. Mike and Steven each pick up a win on the way to the Windy City. We never even leave the lounge car on the entire ride to Chicago.

Once at Union Station in Chicago, our layover is shorter than anticipated because our train was late. Instead of exploring the city, we decide to eat lunch at one of the restaurants in the station and be ready to board the train.

The Amish keep streaming into the station. Kansas Wayne Miller is ramrodding an entire train-car load heading from Chicago to Glenwood Springs, Colorado, for a week. Among many others traveling with Wayne and his family are Floyd and Sharon Lambright, Kenny and Jewel Bontrager and family, Glen and Wanita Chupp, and Eugene and Ruth Yoder. If you are thinking it sounds like a lively bunch, then you're thinking what I'm thinking.

Finally boarding our westward-bound train, the eight of us are directed into a compartment on the lower level. This gives us more solitude and quiet. A couple sits behind us. She is a Quaker and helps us sing a few songs.

Through Illinois and Iowa, we roll through rain and flooded areas. We see storms from the comfort of the lounge car, with Settlers in front of us and friends around us. Life is rough.

Esther has an embarrassing moment during this stretch. We are sitting six at a table to play, and this is a tight squeeze. A slight miscalculation in Esther's balance and a slight roll of the train combine to deposit her into the aisle on her derriere. Ah, the way of the transgressor is hard.

I don't know if she was the one who taped my pillow, but I am confident she didn't try to stop it either. We boys are now catching up.

Steven has the hot hand early at Settlers, and he owns the lead in wins as we retire for the night.

We are looking forward to some of God's magnificent handi-work west of Denver tomorrow morning.

• • •

The weapon of choice, pink tape, is being applied again. This time it is turned outward from our group of eight travelers, and Ora and Lorene Lehman are the victims.

We eight are seated on the lower level of our train car and thus have easy access to everyone's luggage. This is too tempt-ing for the mischievous ones in our bunch. The girls broach the idea, and friend Calvin quickly takes charge. He knows Ora and

Lorene well and expresses his friendly greetings by wrapping and rewrapping their suitcase in pink duct tape.

Ora and Lorene are upstairs and blissfully unaware.

A few hours later, while parked in Denver on this Sunday morning, many of us have had personal devotions. There is great value in communal services though, and a few of us take the opportunity here in our private section of this car to stand in the aisle and exercise our ecclesiastical tendencies. Quite simply, we practice preaching. Only later do we realize the door behind us was open and those on the upper level of the train car heard our sermon. Oops. No shouts of "Amen" or "Hallelujah" reached us.

After we leave Denver, we enjoy the views as our train climbs the mountains west of town. The Moffat Tunnel takes us across the Continental Divide, and we notice the water flowing the other way.

A few hours after the bag-taping episode, I pass through the upper level of our train car on my way to the lounge car. I am hailed. And accused. Ora and Lorene are highly suspicious and interrogate me as I stand in the aisle—innocent as Snow White. Finally they are halfheartedly convinced, and I am allowed to leave without handcuffs. I don't know if they ever did discover who the real culprit was.

We continue our epic battle over the Settlers of Catan game board—right up until it is time to pack up and get off the train in Grand Junction, Colorado.

My friend Lee Essary and his friend Larry are waiting at the train station to transport us to our planned destination of beautiful Ouray, Colorado. Panoramic views surround us as we drive south through Colorado. Passing through a town as we approach Ouray, the girls choose a spot to eat. Dairy Queen. We fellows turn up our noses a bit at this generic choice, and it turns out this DQ doesn't serve many sandwiches. We move on and stop at a Wendy's. We eat there, and it's okay—just like DQ would have been. But we tell the girls that, from here on, any restaurant that is also located in Middlebury or Goshen is off limits. We are traveling to experience the country, not to stay in our cocoon.

While ordering at the Wendy's, Mike and I make a point of asking for chicken fillets. We pronounce it *fill-uts*. The fun is in watching the faces of the workers and imagining them thinking of what an ignorant bunch of hicks we must be. The other enjoyable part of playing ignorant is watching the girls with us become all embarrassed. They just can't see the point of making people think we're backward and dim.

We arrive in Ouray—a charming little town nestled in the mountains. We get situated in our rooms at the Hot Springs Inn, which overlooks the river. Mike and Steven are feeling ambitious and debating whether to climb the nearly vertical mountainside opposite the river from our rooms. I tell them they won't make it more than fifty feet. This is the perfect way to ensure these two fire-eaters will climb it all the way to the top. Calling Mike and Steven competitive is like calling LeBron James a decent basketball player.

They do make it to the top and enjoy the sunset from that viewpoint.

• • •

It is Monday, July 1. The snowballs are flying. The eight of us have ridden in the open back of Chad's jeep from toasty Ouray up here to the top of Imogene Pass (altitude 13,000-plus feet), where it's not so toasty.

We enjoy the view of the ceiling of Colorado and down into Telluride on the opposite side of the pass. At different times on this trip, we pause to imagine how our almighty Creator must have enjoyed creating this widely varied land. And why create such magnificent variety? Certainly not because these mountaintops are good spots to grow corn and beans. Don't you think God created it for the enjoyment and amazement of his children? We like to think so.

Yeah, we enjoy the view, but the wet snow up here is too tempting just to ignore. It flies around—creating some, uh, invigorating moments.

Chad, our jeep tour guide, is greeted here at the top by a tour guide from Telluride. "Hey, Chad, when did you get out of jail?"

Friend Lee Essary later tells us that is one of the favorite lines in the love language of the jeep drivers. Others are: "Boy, the shop sure did a nice job taking the dents out of your jeep after you rolled it last week!" and, Lee's favorite, "Hey, those people you took yesterday, are they out of the hospital yet?"

They say Ouray is the jeep capital of the world. We know that. Emily has told us eleven times.

On the bumpy ride back down to Ouray, Emily suddenly hollers "Elk!" and points down into the green valley to our right. We peer down to a spot beside the creek. Emily goes to great pains to explain exactly where the elk is. Chad even exits the jeep, walks around it, and wants to have a look.

Finally, the sun sweeps out from behind a cloud and illuminates the spot. The "elk" disappears.

Emily is doomed for the rest of the trip to have her spottings followed by questions on the proximity of sunshine.

Touch football is the game that evening at Ouray's spacious town park. Mike, Emily, Neomah, and I manage to defeat Calvin, Steven, Esther, and Mary. Mike snags my pass in the corner of the end zone to clinch it while our two ladies block a hard-charging Steven who was intent on a sack.

Then we play Frisbee football with the same teams. This game is Calvin's specialty, and he guides his team to a decisive victory over us.

Lee and his friend Larry graciously haul us north to the train station the next afternoon. Our time in Ouray is over. Larry asks for our names and the schools where we plan to teach. (Seven of us are teachers.) Larry says he'll be praying for us. This Texan is easy to like.

After arriving and unloading at the train station in Grand Junction, we have time to go get supper. Lee takes a few of us to a nearby Burger King where we purchase food for everyone.

I get a bit creative while preparing Calvin's drink at the soda fountain. Ever put a little bit of everything in your large drink? Calvin has not said a word about it to this day, though. Either the drink was good, or Calvin was loath to give me the satisfaction of hearing him gripe.

Finally we board the train. California, my favorite state to visit, is the next destination. We chase the sun heading out of Colorado.

32

GOLDEN GATE BRIDGE

MICHAEL IS six-foot-four and his skin is quite white. He is the bellhop at our four-star hotel in San Francisco. As we arrive and clamber out of our taxis, Michael greets the eight of us professionally. Upon learning the bellhop's name, our compadre Mike Lambright asks him if he is Michael Jordan.

We fellows snicker. The girls roll their eyes.

The "ignorant act" still often works on complete strangers—such as when we pronounced *jalapeño* with a hard *j* sound and were corrected by another passenger on the train. Strangers still bite, but the four ladies and four gent—er, boys—in our group have been burned often enough that we are very cautious, especially if Lambright is expounding.

Just a few hours ago, though, Mike got me to bite—hard. I'm still trying to spit out the hook. We were still on the train and approaching San Francisco. The Pacific was not in sight but there was a body of water to our right—probably a bay. One could actually see land on the other side. Mike came charging up to my seat. With enthusiastic tones he proclaimed, "Look! The ocean."

Like some naive child, I said exactly what he wanted me to say. "I'm guessing it's actually a bay."

The hearty laugh I heard next is all it took to tell me I had been had.

• • •

We have time yet this evening to stroll a few blocks through downtown San Fran to an Italian restaurant to eat. Walking along the bustling sidewalks as we return to the hotel, Mike "accidentally" collides with a post and falls backward. Remarkably, Steven is just in the right spot to catch him. A passerby checks to see if Mike is okay.

More snickers. More rolled eyes.

Early the next morning, July Fourth, we go on a Big Bus Tour for a hop-on, hop-off, open-top tour of the city. We see Divisadero Street and some of the city office buildings—one of which is where Marilyn Monroe married Joe DiMaggio. We cruise through the famous corner of Haight and Ashbury. The automated tour guide tells us that the reason one of the neighborhoods is named the Tenderloin is because policemen were paid more to work that beat due to the higher crime rate and thus could afford tenderloin instead of cheaper meat.

Golden Gate Park is the first stop where we hop off. The California Academy of Science is located inside this park. We take in the aquarium and planetarium. Also in the Academy of Science is a promotional display for America's Cup, which is an international sailing race to be held in the city this summer. There is a memorable little story included in the display.

The Queen of England was watching the finish of one of the past races. She asked someone who won.

"The Americans, your Majesty."

"Who was second?" the Queen inquired.

"Your Majesty, there is no second place."

• • •

Our next stop is finally the Golden Gate Bridge. We go across and get off on the Marin County side. From there we enjoy the view of the bay, the bridge, and the skyline of San Francisco.

Then we walk across the world-famous Golden Gate Bridge. It is a 1.2 mile trek and we occasionally pause to gaze way down at the waters of the bay or to debate whether we should climb up onto the railing for a more thrilling experience. The ladies with us strongly discourage this and suspect we're *loco*.

Perhaps they have some justification for this.

They say the bridge sways twenty-seven feet side to side in the winds that whistle through here. The determined breeze sweeping in off the Pacific snatches at my hat.

We trot up the steps of the next open-top Big Bus, cruise past the Palace of Fine Arts, and are soon on Lombard Street. Unfortunately, we turn off of Lombard before reaching the crooked part. Lombard's moniker is "the crookedest street in the world," though it isn't, actually.

After looping through downtown, we turn onto Embarcadero, which borders this city's famous piers.

It is jammed. We finally inch past Pier 39, one of the most popular tourist destinations in the country. People are making themselves comfortable along Embarcadero in anticipation of the fireworks show on the bay tonight.

The bus gets back to the terminal too late to connect us to the bus back to our stop at Union Square. So the bus company gives us a courtesy ride. Although we do have to sit in the bottom level, we amuse ourselves quite trippingly.

Mike asks a passerby if this is the bus to San Antonio, and we do a play-by-play of an imaginary basketball game.

Upon reaching our hotel, we reorganize and snatch a taxi down to the piers for the fireworks show. While waiting for the other four in front of the Ferry Building, we have opportunity to observe the river of humanity flowing by. Wow. I don't recall ever seeing such a variety of ethnicities in one location.

The spot we choose is on a pier between the Ferry Building and the Bay Bridge. In the growing darkness, hearing the lap of the bay waters beneath us, we face northward, watching for the fireworks display. The Bay Bridge, beautiful at night with its vertical cables lit up and shimmering, is right behind us.

After the fireworks, the children of Israel head out of Egypt. We move with the stream of people off the pier, across the blocked-off Embarcadero, and we catch taxis back to the hotel. Our companion Steven Miller, who for some inexplicable reason brought his swimming trunks along tonight, gets tired of carrying them. He puts them on. Over his pants. At least it's dark.

We duke it out over some game boards yet before we retire. Calvin and I pad our undefeated record at the game of *Schnicklefritz* (four-player checkers) against Mary and Neomah. Three times. I'm like Steve Kerr playing with Michael Jordan. All I need to do is fill my role and let the superstar carry us to victory.

• • •

The following morning we ride a bus east across the Bay Bridge to Emeryville, where we catch a train. The destination this time? Modesto, California, home of two congregations of German Baptist (GB) Brethren. German Baptists have Anabaptist roots—like we Amish.

Mike makes a prediction before we meet the GBs. He predicts it will be good to fellowship with people who think like we do.

Later we see that he might as well have said the Pacific is a decent-sized mud puddle. None of us has the slightest idea now of how much we will enjoy the warm Christian love these GBs will show us.

33

HOW DO YOU PLAY
BASKETBALL?

MODESTO, CALIFORNIA, spreads across a well-irrigated valley a few hours east of the Pacific Ocean. The town is prospering and growing rapidly—probably due, at least partly, to the proliferation of orchards surrounding it. Beehives and dairy farms also have their niche in the area. This is a land of milk and honey. It is also home to a well-established settlement of German Baptists.

The eight of us Amish youth pull into Modesto on the train in the late forenoon of this sunny July 5. As promised, my friend Lowell Beachler is there to meet us.

After Lowell and company get us settled in, he takes us to the church's community building. There is another GB extended family holding something of a reunion here. There are volleyball nets as well as basketball courts. The Rumbles welcome us warmly, and we help them play volleyball.

After the volleyball game, we boys gravitate toward the basketball court. This is where it gets interesting. These people don't know us, we are thousands of miles from home, and there are ample opportunities for chicanery. This is way too good for friend Mike to resist.

"So what is this game called?"

"Basketball, you say?"

"What is the object of the game?"

"How did you say you score points?"

This is like Henry Ford asking how to put an automobile together.

Mike shoots a few awkward shots underhanded to continue his ignorant act. Then, resigned to teaching us the game, some of the friendly and athletic Rumble men agree to play Mike, Calvin, and me in a three-on-three matchup.

Before we actually get started, Mike does confess to the Rumbles that basketball is his favorite game. Then the three of us manage to defeat them every time. Who would blame the Rumbles for wanting to twist our ears?

We have a good conversation with one of the patriarchs, John Rumble, who serves as a missionary in China. He relates some interesting accounts of his experiences.

John asks us four boys to sing for them. We oblige. I think we owe them that. We stand together and sing the *Lob Lied* to the tune of "Sweet Hour of Prayer." Rumble and company reciprocate by singing for us and send us off with sno-cones.

That evening we enjoy our time around the campfire at Jon and Bev Flora's place where our four ladies are staying. The ice is melting, and our hosts are beginning to realize that some of our number have an ornery streak. We spend time on the important things, too, singing hymns together. Per their request, we sing a verse of our *Lob Lied* in our normal slow fashion.

The next day we awake to a gorgeous Saturday morning in California. Oh, this is pleasant! Lowell and his wife, Doris, take us through Modesto and to the home of their brethren Tim and

Mitzi Frantz. We get a hint of what's in store for us there as we pull in the driveway past a field with Tim's zebra herd in it.

From the back seat, Mike comments on the strange spots that herd of horses has. Calvin, Steven, and I have been burned way too often to even think about rising to that one. But Lowell hasn't.

"Those are zebras," he corrects Mike.

Then Lowell realizes that is exactly what Mike wanted him to say. This eighty-two-year-old, warm Christian man threatens to wrestle Mike down and pound him. He has to grin soon afterward, though.

Tim Frantz greets us and leads us up his shop stairs to his three trophy rooms. Shock and awe. The other boys (who know much more about these matters than I) say Cabela's pales in comparison. An entire stuffed giraffe holds court in a room with an elephant, hippopotamus, rhinoceros, and an alligator. One other entire wall is filled with trophy whitetails. These are right beside the head mount of an albino buffalo. These are all animals the Frantzes have hunted down for a jaw-dropping total of 233 different species, including the ones still coming from the taxidermist.

Mitzi shows us her collection of flow blue china before we leave. There is a youth gathering tonight.

• • •

The local parishioners are gathering. It is a gorgeous Sunday morning in rural California. The German Baptist Brethren's simple, yet roomy, church house is filling up. The goodwill and warm feelings almost bubble as these Christian brothers and sisters assemble.

The body of pews is divided into three sections. We four Amish boys find seats smack-dab in the middle with our newly adopted German Baptist grandfather, Lowell Beachler. He can barely contain his excitement at being in an assembly of saints with us. He is that kind of warm people person.

Many of the GB youth are gathered in the right-hand third of the pews. And they're not all local. Youth camp is set for next week, and youth have arrived from different parts of the country early enough to take in church services and the other doings this weekend. The visitors add a level of excitement to the peaceful, warm, expectant air of camaraderie that usually pervades the beginning of church services.

The service gets underway. We are enjoying the blend of singing, praying, and preaching. Then a slight commotion catches our eye.

Sure enough, it's the four Amish girls coming in late. Emily, Esther, Mary, and Neomah have crossed eight states and traveled thousands of miles. But they forgot to leave their late tendency in Indiana.

They find seats and the service continues. Somehow we force ourselves to eat of the potluck lunch after the services. What a spread! There are delicious foods of all kinds.

There is volleyball and basketball in the afternoon at the community center. By now, most of these sharp Anabaptist cousins of ours have caught on to the ignorant act we Hoosiers occasionally put on about these games. So we just play.

The gathering here is something of a melting pot for these youth from across the country. And we are right in the middle of it. It is fun. Our companions Calvin and Mike end up on the same volleyball team and go undefeated the entire afternoon. Steven and I itch for a shot at them. We give a lot of credit for the stellar record Mike and Calvin carry to the ladies on their team. Steven and I don't get an opportunity today, though. We'll have to wait until Montana.

Another church service is in the works Sunday evening. It is held at the community's other meetinghouse, which was formerly on the outskirts of Modesto. Now the town has grown up around it.

Services have again begun when, guess what, here come the girls. Apple trees still bear apples even if transplanted to California, and these Hoosier girls still have a flair for the dramatic entrance here on the Pacific seaboard. To my knowledge, they are the only Amish people who have ever been late to church twice in one day.

The sermons God gives us tonight are memorable. Vince Tye is the first speaker. As a young man, he had been schooling to be a lawyer when he converted to the German Baptists. Now he is a minister. His keen mind is evident as we hear a very academic, nuts-and-bolts talk on America's infrastructure—not the infrastructure that includes roads and bridges.

In the main message, we get perhaps the most vivid word picture we've ever heard on heaven and hell. This minister has done his research, and God gives us a remarkable sermon through him.

There is another youth gathering tonight before we head to bed in anticipation of our jaunt to the über-beautiful Yosemite tomorrow.

34

CONQUERING UPPER YOSEMITE FALLS

IT'S BEEN CALLING to me, Yosemite Falls has. We were here a while ago, hiked partway up to the top of the beautiful mountaintop falls—just enough to get a tantalizing view—and had to turn back. I've wanted to finish the job ever since.

Now it's July, and Yosemite Falls finally appears again through the window of our rented white Ford van. This winding, up-and-down road has led us into Yosemite Valley once more.

We have some planning to do. I do not want to leave this place again without having conquered the "very strenuous" Upper Yosemite Falls trail. We drop Calvin off at an information station to do some investigating—the man is a whiz with maps—and the rest of us go get settled in our tent cabins.

Calvin comes back, and we put together a game plan. We'll save Upper Yosemite Falls for tomorrow morning. This afternoon we'll hike the "strenuous" 1.5 miles up to Vernal Falls, then drive up to Glacier Point tonight.

The nine dwarves go marching up the Vernal Falls Trail. Eight of us are Amish from Indiana. Steve Rapp is a single, German Baptist man from Washington, who was kind enough to accompany us and do our driving.

Many other people are on this trail with us. They comprise a cross section of the peoples of the world. Here among all these strangers, some personalities emerge from our group. For instance, if we nine are walking single file and the leader seems to stumble, we come to the understanding that the other eight are also to stumble at the exact same point. It's quite interesting to note the reactions of strangers who witness our simulated stumbling.

Mike and I tend to leave the trail if we see something inviting off to the side somewhere. One such point is the bottom of Vernal Falls. A slight trail leads down toward the base and away from the well-beaten stone stairway we've been on. The two dumb—I mean bravest—ones in our group follow the little path. It winds around rocks and down toward the pool at the bottom of the falls.

The wind and mist from the thundering impact of the water get stronger and wetter as we get closer. It buffets us. Finally, it is hard both to see and to catch our breath, and we turn back. We have gotten soaked, but we did get close enough to see the rainbow hanging in the mist. It was worth it.

We continue up the rock stairway and finally reach the top of Vernal Falls and the large, crystal-clear pool a bit upstream. Here we dry out for a bit and soak up some sun.

Well, some of us dry out. Mary tosses water on me despite my dire warnings against it. This water is snow melt and shockingly cold. I deposit Mary into the pool.

After hiking back down and eating supper, we clamber into the van and set out for Glacier Point. If we were a murder of crows instead of a flock of turkeys, it would take probably three minutes to get up to Glacier Point from our campground in

Yosemite Valley. As it is, we have an hour's drive out of the valley, around the mountain, and up to Glacier Point. Then we walk from the parking lot on up the trail and out to the very point. *Unverständich.*

There we are rewarded with one of the more breathtaking views I've seen in all my travels. The point overlooks Yosemite Valley thousands of feet below. The lights of the valley sparkle up through the dusk. "A thing of beauty is a joy forever," the poet said. There will be joy as long as the memory of this scene remains in our hearts.

As an added bonus, an amateur astronomer camped out on the point lets us take a peek through his telescope, which he has trained on Saturn. The rings are vivid.

On the drive back down, we are serenaded by Steven's story of a lonely bachelor and Calvin's preaching.

Then we return to our tent cabins and retire. Upper Yosemite Falls awaits.

• • •

Today is the day. Upper Yosemite Falls is "just over there" when we wake in our tent cabins and the eight of us plan to go admire it—from the top.

We rise early on this July morning, eat a hearty breakfast at the Camp Curry restaurant in Yosemite Valley, and hop on the shuttle to the trailhead.

We enter the trees at the base of the trail and start gaining altitude pronto. When the writers of the guidebook called this trail "very strenuous," they weren't joking.

Dozens of switchbacks make up the lion's share of this trail. Calvin volunteers to carry Steven's pack for a bit. Nice guy.

When Calvin returns it, there is a large rock hidden in the bottom of it. Steven soon elects to jettison the rock.

During one rest, we are pleased to meet Bush. Kenny "Bush" Miller of Millersburg, Indiana, that is, and his compadre, Andrew Jones of Middlebury, Indiana. We had no idea they were in the area. They join us for our climb.

Up, up, and, um, up we go. This is a sweat-inducing, laboring grind. The view is gorgeous though, especially at the occasional lookout points we come to, and with a group of friends like this, it is pleasurable. The best part is the reward we anticipate at the top. It could remind one of the Christian walk.

The climb back and forth up the mountainside continues. The ladies of our group finally tell us they want to take more time. We six gents go on ahead.

We finally attain the summit. A beautiful series of pools rewards us here. The stream forms these pools as it flows toward the mountainside and the falls.

Boys will be boys—even on a mountaintop in California. The pools beckon, and many of us dive into the icy, clear water for a, shall we say, invigorating swim.

After refueling with some snacks, I pick my way out to the overlook above the falls. Crawling flat on my stomach, I inch out to the edge of the flat rock and peer down onto the falls and the drop of 2,425 feet. I get a magnificent view of God's handiwork in sun-splashed Yosemite Valley. Mist floats up and forms a rainbow. Is this place ever a jewel!

Steve, our German Baptist driver, Calvin, Bush, Andrew, and I elect to go the short distance up to the very top overlook here. We wouldn't want to miss anything. We've climbed this 3.6-mile trail anyway. Might as well see it all.

Then we head back down to the valley floor. Calvin and I get separated from the others, and when we make it back down, we visit the gift shop before returning to our rented van.

Mike and Steven got it into their heads to see how fast they could make the descent. They do it in something like fifty-five minutes. Maybe the altitude affected their brains.

When everybody is back at the van, we load up and go visit the grove of giant sequoias at the south end of Yosemite. We marvel at these tremendous trees, at least one of which is most of two millennia old.

Then we leave Yosemite and make for "home": the German Baptist community in Modesto, California.

35

FINAL LEGS OF THE BEST WEST QUEST

THE PACIFIC IS bitterly, bitingly, utterly cold. It is so frigid that once we immerse ourselves the water actually numbs us and we are able to enjoy the surf. We just barely feel it anymore.

We returned from Yosemite yesterday to our German Baptist friends in Modesto, California. Today they have chauffeured us eight Amish youth to the coast. This is the next leg of our seventeen-day exploration through the West. Today we've visited the redwood forest in Santa Cruz, grabbed a bite to eat at the pier, and are now at Sunset Beach.

The beach is almost deserted, perhaps due to the overcast weather and the less-than-cozy temperature. Our football flies around, we find some sand dollars and shells, then vamoose.

Back in Modesto, Jon Flora gives us supper at a local buffet; Lowell Beachler gives us a tearful, touching goodbye; and they both give us a lift to the train station.

At the station, we hold hands. We say a prayer. We sing a few songs. The warm connection we feel with these fellow Anabaptists is praiseworthy. I think maybe this is how brothers and sisters in Christ are supposed to—are privileged to—feel.

• • •

Midnight in Sacramento. This is where we switch trains. We board the Coast Starlight here for the journey up the West Coast. Montana, here we come. The Big Sky State will never be the same.

Oregon is lush. Portland is sunny. Then we cross the mighty Columbia River and turn eastward. We will be traveling along the famous Columbia for a while. I see Lewis and Clark with Sacagawea—in my mind's eye, that is.

It is while traveling along the Columbia that we meet up with Lime and Bizzy. Lime shows us pictures of a 3-D Settlers of Catan gameboard he developed. He must be a fanatic.

Lime and his girlfriend, Bizzy, gather around a table in the lounge car with us four Amish lads. The Settlers battle begins. Poor Lime and Bizzy. They have obviously played before, but perhaps not against players as aggressive as we are. The two newcomers get creamed as Calvin takes both games.

• • •

Montana. Scotty (he pronounces it *Scawty*) picks us up in Whitefish and delivers us to the town of St. Ignatius. We plan to go canoeing later today, and the girls buy a big new water gun on the way down. They always did have a hard time with the concept of not biting off more than they can chew.

A pickup with a livestock trailer hauls us to our put-in spot. We scoot down a steep grassy bank and glide onto the sparkling, clear, green Flathead River.

The canoeing is delightful. The water is merely cool, not unpleasantly cold. We can see the bottom of the river much of the time, even if the water is as deep as ten feet in some places.

Emily and Esther, though they were warned against it, are soon spraying us with their new water gun. After a few tries, Mike and I dump them and appropriate the offending water blaster. Mike soon employs the gun against Steven. Steven promptly abandons his canoe, swims over, and dumps us. Somewhere the girls are laughing.

• • •

I am tired of losing. In California a few days ago, Mike and Calvin ran the table with their volleyball team, going undefeated at the expense of Steven and me. Today, while canoeing on the river in Montana, Steven got the best of Mike and me in the dumping battle. And tonight while supping at Arlene Bontrager's house here in St. Ignatius, Montana, I was utterly thrashed by Arlene in a verbal duel. She had a trump card for every one of my comebacks. Arlene obviously shares the quick wit of her sister, Marlene (Delmar) Miller, of Topeka, Indiana.

All these, um, battles are in fun, of course. I just wouldn't mind winning one every now and again.

Frothing at the lips, Steven and I are anticipating the volleyball game in Arlene's front yard after supper. We plan to make sure Mike and Calvin are on the other team.

We do, and we also end up with another hitter, a young man named Reuben, and his wife, Rachel, on our team, as well as our comrade Esther and a local lass named Ann. To be fair, our teammates give us a slight advantage.

All asterisks aside, the undefeated record is quickly blemished. Three times in a row. Tee-hee. We're relieved to have that monkey off our backs. Reuben and Rachel then leave, and Mike and Calvin win a few.

• • •

St. Ignatius is nestled on the eastern portion of broad Mission Valley, which lies on the west side of a snowcapped mountain range. The roads in this picturesque community, while fairly straight and flat, all slope uphill as they go east toward the looming mountains.

Tomorrow is a big day for the Amish community here. They are hosting their annual school fundraising auction—and a large one it looks to be. Calvin and I plan to help with it.

We four boys pedal the few miles back to the house of Ed and Brenda Beachy, our hospitable hosts.

• • •

Saturday is auction day. Jake Yoder, the lead auctioneer, assigns Calvin and me to the same ring. We spend much of the day working together, which is fun. Calvin cracks me up once while I am selling, though, and I am forced to pause while I get over my laughing fit. The comical sap.

Jake lets me sell in the furniture ring, and Ed and Brenda, the quilt bosses, give me a shift in the quilt tent, too. They bless me with the opportunity to sell the hyped "Moon Glow" quilt.

This striking, black-and-green piece of art sells for $2,000. This is quite high, though another quilt made by a local widow sold earlier for almost $4,000. The community is astounded. Ed and Brenda say it is an excellent sale.

This evening the locals take us through the bison range, a huge drive-through wild animal park. Cousin Eric quickly catches onto our game of purposely mispronouncing words, and we get driver Scotty badly on *photographer*.

We play some basketball at Ed's before turning in for the night.

Sunday morning we gather for church at the community meetinghouse. The Indiana girls, Emily, Esther, Mary, and Neomah, are on time. This is a pleasant change. The song leaders ask us four Hoosier boys to lead the *Lob Lied*. We do so. Christy T. Yoder of Vevay, Indiana, preaches the first sermon, a local reads Scripture, and John Henry Troyer of Ohio has the main part. The contributions come from sea to shining sea. God blesses us with an interesting sermon.

All of us travelers gather at Ed and Brenda's in their gorgeous backyard, along with some other locals, for supper in the evening. We enjoy a fine meal and some games, skits, and singing. The northern lights appear before we retire. The evening is a pleasant conclusion to our Montana visit.

• • •

Oh, Montana. Wherefore art thou so distant from Indiana?

California is still higher on my favorite states list, but one could make a solid case for the big skies, rolling green plains, and rugged mountain beauty of Montana.

A driver hauls the eight of us from St. Ignatius to the train station in Whitefish. We'll be traveling east from here on out.

Mark Twain once said, "Travel is fatal to prejudice, bigotry, and narrow-mindedness, many of our people need it sorely on these accounts." I imagine some of the strangers we've met on this seventeen-day trek would wholeheartedly agree with that.

Throughout this entire trip, we eight—well, the four boys at least—have enjoyed catching strangers off guard with unorthodox pronunciations and generally acting ignorant. It's while boarding the train in Whitefish that a stranger catches me unaware. Let me explain.

Many people, when happy, will show it by whistling, humming a tune, or singing a song. I am just as apt to exhibit my happiness to those around me by breaking into an auction chant. My friends are used to it. My siblings are annoyed by it. Strangers are confused by it.

I bring up the rear as our eight climb the stairs inside the train car just after boarding. Another man is behind me. Absentmindedly, I launch into an auction chant while filing down the aisle.

The man behind me gets my attention and reassures me. "Just keep taking your medication," he says without a hint of a smile. "It will be all right."

I've heard that line eighty-one times since then from my siblings.

We enjoy God's scenery in Montana from the train today. As usual, we spend quite a bit of time in the lounge car playing games. We play more chess and *Schnicklefritz* the rest of the way and less Settlers of Catan.

We have played between forty and fifty Settlers games on this trip already. Mike Lambright has sewn up the Settlers title, garnering thirteen wins. My nine is good for—oops—"Your Majesty," they said to the Queen, "there is no second place."

Schnicklefritz is a relatively new game much like a two-on-two checkers match. I play Watson to Calvin's Sherlock Holmes and we stay undefeated on this jaunt, winning all six of our games.

Another train traveler, also named Mike, joins us for some chess. The man plays above our level and wins every time, except once. Sherlock pulls a quick four-move checkmate on him. Mike is not satisfied until he has played Calvin again and settled the score.

Our train runs behind schedule, and we are hours late getting into Chicago. Amtrak feeds us a complimentary supper on the train.

Upon arriving in the Windy City, instead of having a three-hour layover, our eastbound train is ready for us. We board that one directly and are soon on the last leg of our excursion. We're going home.

36

HOW THE CATFISH
CLEANS HIS TEETH

IF MY FISHLINE is unbreakable, they just pull the whole fishing pole into the pond!"

Windy Willy is at it again. He is telling tall tales with a flair that is unmatched anywhere in these parts. If the sparkles in the eyes of Willy's listeners are any indication, these tales are entertaining many others besides just Willy.

As Windy Willy gets into the heart of his fish story, his listeners unconsciously lean in and gather a bit closer. These stories have a reputation much more for being entertaining than for having any basis in actual fact. You see, Willy's stories are so wild that there is little danger of anyone actually believing them.

The scene is the campfire at the annual neighborhood summer social. Someone gets Willy started on the catfish in his farm pond, and now there is no telling what will come forth.

The neighborhood boys, who had been industriously catching fireflies, abandon that task and scoot to the campfire when they hear that Windy Willy is telling stories again. The young girls who had been sitting in a huddle off to the side, whispering, giggling, and whatever else girls do when they get together, likewise scamper to within earshot of Willy. He is going full tilt about his catfish.

"Well, after I'd lost three fishing poles and umpteen lines to the buggers, I decided it's time to teach 'em a lesson," Willy continues. "I got out Bill and Dan, my big Belgian team that weighed a ton apiece. I hooked up those big boys to a metal evener fastened to a log chain. I extended that chain out a ways, put my bait right on that big old chain hook, and tossed it into the water. Yes sir, it was high time to show these catfish who is boss."

Willy pauses for a second and soaks up the environment in this moment of suspense. The wide, shining eyes and bated breath of his audience serve to add fuel to Willy's storytelling fire.

"I didn't have long to wait. A catfish grabbed a hold of that fishline and took off for the other end. That's where things got really ugly. I told Bill and Dan "giddap" and figured they'd pull a nice catfish onto the bank for me.

"Alas, it was not to be. The chain got very tight, held for one fateful moment, and then started going the wrong way. The wrong way! Those catfish pulled my best Belgian team right into the pond!"

Here Willy pauses as if in regret. "It was one of the saddest times in my life. Bill and Dan got sucked under the surface, and I never saw them again."

Now someone asks, half-seriously, "What do you think happened to the horses?"

Windy Willy grimaces. "I do have one clue. The next day I went back to see if I could find any trace of them. All I saw was one solitary catfish. He was slowly swimming through the shallows, picking meat out of his teeth with my metal evener."

37

HAY BALES

VOLTAIRE, the French thinker, said, "Work keeps at bay three great evils: boredom, vice, and need."

Well, I'm not bored now.

Sweat rolls down my face. I wipe it hastily while I charge from the back of the moving hay wagon to the front. The goal is to yank the next bale onto the wagon before it tumbles off the chute and onto the ground because the baler is shoving the next bale through. Blisters are forming.

Sister Emily is the teamster handling the four horses pulling the baler and attached wagon. Her natural horsemanship stands her in good stead (most of the time) as she guides the caravan in circles, gobbling up the rows of hay.

• • •

Haybaling is a bit of an art. The hay must be dried so as not to rot after being compressed into bales. However, the savvy farmer doesn't want his hay so dry that it loses nutritional value and palatability for his stock. The whole operation becomes a bit of a juggling act, including watching the weather forecast for an idea of when it will be sunny, cloudy, or (look out!) rainy. The farmer needs a feel for when the hay is ripe to cut, dry enough to rake into rows, then dry enough to bale. Experience helps.

My dad, he of the uncanny haying instincts, is not home today. The final decisions are up to me. Some of our ten acres was cut yesterday, some two days ago. Will all of it be fit to bale today? Rain is forecast for tomorrow. It would be a comfort to have it all in the barn.

I check both parts of the field. There is little doubt that the first will be ready. The second is iffy. I decide. We'll rake the first part straightaway and wait just a bit to rake the rest. Then we'll try to bale it all.

Sisters Emily and Ramah rake while I prep our baler. This is the first time it will be used this season, so I gas it up, check that it has twine, and grease it.

The girls bring their teams to the barn from across the road where they had been raking. We eat a quick lunch. Then it's time to hit it.

I used to dread haying time. Now it's almost a rush, if things click. Emily and Ramah go back to the field to rake the second part while Mom, Grace, and I harness and hitch the big four-horse team to the baler. A few empty wagons bring up the rear as our procession crosses the road, makes its way back along the driveway between the neighbors' houses, and enters the field.

Mom takes Emily's spot on the rake, and Emily grabs the lines at the head of the baling column. We came. We saw. We baled.

We begin with one of the outside rounds. My job on the wagon is to monitor the quality and weight of the bales, make adjustments to the baler accordingly, and stack the bales on the moving wagon. Any farm-raised boy can do this stacking, but it is still gratifying to see a well-balanced load rise on the wagon as I stack the bales like pieces in a puzzle.

Emily's job—steering the horses pulling the baler—while not so physically strenuous, still takes a level of skill, especially on the "inside-out" left turns we're making on this first round. As we go past one corner, I see that Emily didn't get it all. She left hay lying on the ground, just in case Job would come through here and need some to feed his camels. I think there's enough. I don't say that out loud to Emily. Uh-uh. Not yet.

Emily does guide the baler well, though, and gets most of the hay gobbled up. She really is a good horsewoman. This just makes it more fun when she messes up occasionally.

We finish the outside round, switching wagons as they are filled, and point the baler toward the middle of the field. Emily raked this part earlier today and didn't listen—er, she misunderstood—er, we had a miscommunication about—how to rake it. Bottom line: a few of the rows in the middle are thicker than they should be. Now Emily has to hold the horses back to a slow walk and even stop them sometimes so the baler can keep up.

There is nothing slow about the rear of the baler, though. With all this hay going in its mouth, our trusty New Holland is kicking out bales at a rapid clip. I have to scramble to keep up on the wagon.

At one point, the raked row is actually so wide the baler can't reach all the hay. I jump down and quickly help Emily fix the problem. I do mention to my sister how unfortunate it is that she can't blame someone else for the raking job. Promptly I get back on the wagon. No point in giving Emily time to think of a retort.

We do get finished, though, and when darkness has fallen, all the hay is baled. Truly, it was hard work. Strange how good it feels.

38

THE KANSAS ANDY BOYS
STRIKE AGAIN

THE SCENE IS a common one in Amish life. Two horses are trotting docilely, pulling buggies in opposite directions down a country road, still a hundred yards apart. There appears to be nothing unusual in the whole scenario.

When the Kansas Andy boys are occupying one buggy, though, anything can and likely will happen.

• • •

Kansas Andy's Henry, in the passenger seat, has his binoculars trained on the oncoming buggy, and Sammy and Mose are becoming impatient. "Can't you tell who it is yet?"

"I think . . ." Henry answers slowly. "Yes, it's Bill's Lonnie!"

"Perfect!" The boys are almost gleeful as they scramble off the seat of the enclosed buggy and kneel in front of the box under cover of the dash. To anyone meeting them on the road, the buggy appears empty.

The ditch-side curtain is left open at the bottom so Sammy, the driver, can keep his bearings while hunkered down so low.

Henry, Sammy, and Mose had determined to spice up their routine buggy trip to town by toying with their fellow travelers.

Getting a chance to play a prank on neighbor Lonnie is much better than they had dared to wish for. The trio had long since deemed Lonnie responsible for the rooster painted neon orange that had shown up in their barn, as well as the mysterious crop of golf balls just a few inches under the surface of their garden that came boiling to the top when Mose went through with the tiller.

The boys also suspected, though they weren't sure, that Lonnie had been responsible for every clock in the house being an hour fast the morning after the youth hymn singing last winter. Henry and Sammy, who work in town, were an hour early for work that morning and have been eagerly waiting for a chance to catch Lonnie when he's vulnerable. Now they have it—if Lonnie takes the bait.

The pranksters huddle, invisible and holding their breath, against the dash of the buggy. They listen to the approaching horse's hoofbeats, now close, now right beside them, now just past.

Quickly and carefully Sammy eases up onto the seat and glances in the mirror. "Yes! He's stopping," Sammy hisses to his brothers. "Now watch how you get up. Do not get in front of the windows."

A driverless horse and carriage is a hazard to the horse, to the carriage, to fellow travelers, and to any fences in the vicinity. Amish children are taught from a young age that such loose horses must be quickly corralled, thereby preventing further damage. Lonnie is no exception. When he sees his neighbor's team running "loose" down the road, he wastes no time.

Quickly he halts his horse, hands the lines to his brother, and jumps out of his own buggy to begin sprinting after the runaway.

Sammy and company, now back on the buggy seat, though careful not to show themselves, have already eased the whip out the front of the buggy. With only an occasional glance in the mirror, they can keep track of Lonnie's progress as he tries to catch up.

The brothers allow Lonnie to get within a tantalizing ten feet of the rear of the buggy before gently tapping the rump of their horse with the whip. Trigger obligingly speeds up, and Lonnie, legs pumping determinedly, loses fifty strides.

Now the grinning lads watch the mirror carefully. What will Lonnie do? They can almost hear the turmoil going on under Lonnie's straw hat.

It would be tempting to give up. Stop and use a phone. Should I? But no, the highway is just three-quarters of a mile farther. That horse needs to be stopped now. . . . Maybe he'll slow down again. Maybe . . .

Lonnie steels himself and lengthens his stride just a bit more. His breath begins to come in tearing gasps. The sweat starts to run down his back. And he begins to catch up to the buggy in front of him.

Now the gap is eighty feet, now fifty, now fifteen, now he is within just a few strides of the elusive carriage, and there it goes again!

For some reason, the horse out front has decided now to quicken the pace. Now, when victory was almost within his grasp. Now, when his grueling sprint was almost over. The gap widens again.

Lonnie feels like collapsing on the pavement. The highway with its heavy traffic is closer yet, though, and Lonnie is made of stern stuff. He grits his teeth, tosses his hat to the side, and extracts one more effort from deep inside himself.

The boys in the buggy are shaking with mirth and are now more boldly peeking into the mirrors. They see the sweat blotches on Lonnie's shirt, the set of his shoulders, and the determination of his stride. When the whites of Lonnie's pained eyes come into plain view, it is all the passengers can do to restrain themselves from shouting in laughter.

Lonnie makes a few final staggering strides around the buggy and grasps the horse by the bridle. "Whoa!" he gasps in a quavering voice. He is utterly spent. Having stopped the horse, Lonnie bends over, sides heaving, sweat dripping, struggling only to regain some oxygen and equilibrium.

A voice floats out of the carriage behind him, cool and collected as you please. "Well hello, Lonnie, what's the problem?"

Lonnie's heaving shoulders stiffen noticeably, and he turns slowly. That buggy, he was sure, had been empty. But that voice: it sounds familiar.

As Lonnie turns, three wide-eyed, querying, and innocent faces peer back at him. The Kansas Andy boys would love to pull one more over on Lonnie and have him think it was all an innocent mistake.

Lonnie is not deceived for an instant. He knows foxes don't sit in henhouses discussing the stock market, and he knows the Kansas Andy boys' buggy didn't accidentally appear empty.

"You ornery *clowns*." Lonnie puts all the feeling he can muster into the last word, drops his hand from the bridle, and begins the long walk back to his own carriage.

39

CANOE CHIVALRY

ESTHER LEHMAN begins her day of canoeing with a splash. She and my sister Emily have just entered the water—in fact, Esther is still not actually seated in her vessel. A few seconds after pushing off from the beach, they are floating broadside past our still-beached canoe. We're ready though, and I am seated in the bow. Levi Zook of Pennsylvania, a good friend, gives our canoe a hefty shove as is necessary to get started. Sadly for the Double E swim team, they are directly in front of us and absorb a jarring blow from the nose of our ship. Emily, who is seated, rides it out with only a few yelps. Esther is not so fortunate.

Anyone who has tried standing in a canoe knows how difficult it is to retain balance. When you throw in a surprise jolt—kiss it goodbye.

The water is shallow enough, so Esther's hand touches the bottom and she only falls halfway out; therefore, she retains her dry status. We help the girls get situated again in their shiny red canoe. Levi and I will end up doing quite a bit of "helping" today.

• • •

Ten canoes carry twenty of us twentysomethings down the Pigeon River out of Mongo. About half of us are Hoosiers; the rest hail from Pennsylvania.

We do not stay dry for very long. Some of these gents have come packing heat—namely, water guns, which they quickly employ. Levi and I, unfortunately, have no water gun and fall victim to the whims of the shooters.

Junior Beiler is especially lethal. He purchased a three-foot-long red Water Blaster at the Trading Post before we embarked. Never have I seen a water gun like it. The Blaster shoots great streams of water for great distances, and Junior quickly gets it into play. Levi and I are almost helpless against Junior's onslaught, and we promptly plot to snatch the Big Red Nuisance. We get it done, too, by sneaking up on Junior's canoe while he and companion Eli are preoccupied.

Levi confiscates the prized weapon, and it has a home in our canoe for a while.

Staying dry is especially hard for gentlemen like Levi and me. There are four canoes with pairs of girls in them. For some reason, it seems that whenever the girls have a mishap and their canoe dumps, Levi and I happen to be close by. Being chivalrous, Levi and I often get out of our canoe, wade the distance to the dumped vessel, and help them get it seaworthy again. Levi and I get wet, but we still feel it's the right thing to do.

The Double E swim team, Esther and Emily, has an especially hard time staying afloat. They seem to spend almost as much time in the river as in their canoe. Levi and I help them several times.

Just before the stop for our picnic lunch, we are, uh, nearby when Neomah and Becky dump. Since the water is too deep to wade, we ask them to hang on to their waterlogged canoe and our dry one. Levi and I huff and puff and tow them the rest of the way to the picnic site. Our chivalry is proving exhausting.

While preparing to eat the tasty picnic lunch that captain Steven Miller has brought along, Levi proclaims that everyone is fortunate that he and I are along. He is referring to the fact that we have assisted every one of the ladies' canoes out of distress.

They do not clap. They do not cheer. They do not give us a medal. Why do our best efforts sometimes go unrewarded?

40

BUCKET LIST

THE INSTRUCTIONS in second grade's spelling workbook say, "Write down four things you want to do yet today."

We discuss it in class, the four second graders and I. When each youngster is done expressing himself, the lone girl asks me, "What did you write down?"

I explain that while I didn't write it down, I do want to do some things, including having a cup of coffee (she wrinkled her nose), going to an auction, and reading a book.

The young lady gets me thinking. What if the question had been, "What do you want to do yet in your *life*?" What would I say to that?

Whenever one's thoughts turn to dying, of course we must think of our only, our rock-solid true hope, Jesus Christ. By believing in Him, then living his message of love, we have no reason to fear death. Indeed, we may look forward to it.

The feeling also remains that, regardless of what we do here that brings us pleasure, it will not even compare to what God has prepared for us.

With that said, there are a few things I'd enjoy doing before I fall asleep for the last time.

Can you imagine a place more fascinating to visit than the Holy Land? What country on earth has more earthshaking events in its history than Israel? I'd like to cross the Sea of Galilee in a small boat. I want to wade in the Jordan River—especially where John baptized Jesus. I want to walk the road to Damascus and explore the Garden of Gethsemane. And I want to climb Calvary and lay my fingers on the spot where the cross stood and where the bridge was built between a perfect God and imperfect man.

• • •

While I'm abroad, the number two spot on my travel list is the Yorkshire Dales. James Herriot kindled a fire in my heart for them in his books about his veterinary life in the Dales. Tall green hills have always drawn me anyway.

The other travel desire that smolders within me, more so when I'm a bit stressed, is to "buy a one-way ticket on a west-bound train." Just cut loose. I'll decide where later—maybe when I'm on the broad expanse of Dakota prairie or under Montana's huge blue sky. Maybe I won't know till I'm in the lush meadows of Oregon or traveling the green fertile hills and valleys of California. I'll decide then.

Yeah, that'll be soon enough.

• • •

Somehow that traveling has to be financially supported, though. And why not do that from home, where I have two jobs I love?

There are a few things I'd like to experience from those two before I go.

As an auctioneer, I am truly beginning to live my childhood dream. It's really happening. I get to sell and people pay me for it. I am blessed.

The big dream remains in front of me, still. Someday I want to sit on the block in a packed auction barn with an electric atmosphere. I want to have high-dollar horses going through the sale ring. And I want to sing my song while thousands follow along.

My rewards from teaching have been mostly in the present—the sweet note and grin from a third grader, the pearl of a poem by the hand of an eighth grader. Maybe someday, though, I'd like to sit under a sermon by one of "my boys" and feel maybe, just maybe, God used me to help the preacher understand the German Scripture that is inspiring him.

Someday, I want to hear a mother reading to the child on her lap, love of literature and a good story evident both in the mother's rising and falling voice and in the child's gleaming eyes. I'd like to feel that, perhaps, I helped kindle that love of reading in the mother and that the torch is now being passed to her child.

There's no telling where it will lead.

FAQS ABOUT THE AMISH:

THE AUTHOR ANSWERS

Author Loren Beachy answers some frequently asked questions about Amish life, faith, and culture.

1. Do the Amish pay taxes?

There are only two things certain in life . . .

Yes, we Amish pay taxes as much as the next person. The myth that we do not pay taxes is a bit grievous, since we believe in following the New Testament's teachings on submitting to the government whenever it doesn't violate biblical principles.

Jesus said, "Render therefore unto Caesar the things which are Caesar's" (Matthew 22:21). I imagine he also meant Uncle Sam.

With all that said, there may be small groups of Amish that choose to be ultra-conservative. If so, they live off the beaten path somewhere, shun Social Security numbers, deal only in cash, and, as far as the government is concerned, may not even exist. I cannot speak for these groups since I have so little information. They are in the distinct minority.

2. Do the Amish use banks and debit cards?

Yes. Throughout the country there is a great degree of variation in how conservative groups of Amish choose to be. Some of the more conservative may not use debit cards, but to the best of my knowledge, almost all Amish use banks. Throughout my area in Indiana, debit cards are fairly prevalent.

3. Do the Amish vote?

As a rule, no. We believe we can help our government more by praying for them than by casting one vote. And we do want to pray for our leaders. (See 1 Timothy 2:2.)

Separation of church and state is an important part of the church's history, and we desire to be citizens of an eternal kingdom much more than an earthly one—thus, the practice of keeping participation in government at arm's length. With this said, there are groups of Amish that choose to vote in local elections, but not in this area.

4. What determines whether the men do or don't wear beards?

In our community, a man will grow a beard once he is married. Not buying razors saves money that he now needs to support a wife.

All jokes aside, originally an Amish young man would grow a beard as soon as he joined the church, regardless of marital status. This is part of our nonconformed culture, much like plain clothes. Through some drift, perhaps, it is now common in many areas to wait until one is married to grow facial hair. In some communities though, men do begin sooner.

5. *What is the role of the bishop in the communities, and how is he chosen?*

I asked Grandpa Miller, a retired bishop, about this one. He responded (and I quote): "A bishop shall be a shepherd to his flock and lead them in preaching the plan of salvation, in baptisms, weddings, and funerals. They are ordained by lot, chosen by God as in Acts 1:23-26."

In my young life, I have lived in churches under three different bishops and have yet to experience a harsh one. People are people and styles and interpretations will vary, but I think it is safe to say there are many more George Washingtons out there than Fidel Castros. It should be noted that although a bishop is ordained to lead the church, there are no decisions on church policy made without the unanimous vote of the members.

6. *Why can the Amish have phones for business or in an outbuilding but not in their homes?*

I politely object to the word *can* in that question. We *choose* not to have phones in our homes or in our pockets, because we fear they will disrupt our family life and lead us away from values we hold dear. We realize we need to make some concessions in order to function in the world, and it has seemed to work well to have a phone slightly separated from the home.

The growing use of cell phones by some Amish is a concern to many and is an issue being sorted through at the present. Again, degrees of conservatism vary.

7. Why do Amish children drop out of school in the eighth grade?

We Amish aim to provide an education that enables a person to earn a living. We believe that an eighth-grade education is sufficient to do this. So far, through all the years, this belief has proven true.

It is felt that higher education tends to lead away from our simple, nonconformed lifestyle. Therefore, we avoid it.

8. Why do the Amish not have their photos taken? Are there exceptions, such as identification cards/passports?

I asked Grandpa Miller for help here. He told me, "We have discouraged photos using one of the Ten Commandments. 'Thou shalt not make unto thee any graven image, or any likeness of any thing that is in heaven above, or that is in the earth beneath, or that is in the water under the earth' (Exodus 20:4). We were granted non-photo IDs but they are no longer available."

He also added that a member of the steering committee was working to find an alternative to photo IDs. If he is unsuccessful, the issue may be revisited out of sheer necessity.

Use of all photos is not strictly shunned in our community, but photos of people are not for display.

9. Why are there so many sects of the Amish and differences in which rules they will follow?

This is an excellent question and may be best answered with, "Because we're human." I think all Amish would agree that we need a line—the clearer the better—in order to keep us nonconformed to the world. Where exactly to draw the line, though? That is where many differences of opinion come into play.

The ideal situation might be that all Amish would agree on all issues and we would have uniform standards across the world. Doesn't happen. It probably never will on this side of the grave. In the meantime, by the grace of God, we'll strive to understand, respect, and love all people as Jesus taught.

10. *What is* **Rumspringa?**

Rumspringa interpreted literally means "running around." What it *really* means and how Hollywood and the media have at times portrayed it are two different things. Shocking, isn't it? Chuckle.

Rumspringa is the period of time when a youth "runs around" with other youth to social functions, hymn singings, recreational sports, et cetera. In the process, he often meets a partner, courts her, and gets married, abruptly ending the "running around."

It is not intended to be a time of partying or other wild excesses. Most of the time, for about 85 percent of the youth, it isn't. Amish teenagers, though, are much like any other teenagers. Sometimes they suddenly think they know much more than their parents and go against their parents' wishes in things they choose to do or have. Some parents permit this. Very few encourage it.

It should be emphasized, though, that while rebellious youth youth may get the headlines, they are distinctly in the minority.

11. *What do you think of Amish-themed reality TV shows?*

Well, I don't see much of them. The little I have seen and heard has appeared to be pretty much fictionalized or unrealistic. The mentality of *Amish Mafia* is so far from Christ's teaching of nonresistance and turning the other cheek as to be ridiculous. No, oftentimes we don't live up to Christ's standards as well as we would wish—we're human. But striking back with force is at the opposite end of the spectrum.

12. Who are your favorite Amish authors?

Elmo Stoll and Daniel Miller. They use their heaps of God-given talent to make their stories accurate and, perhaps almost as importantly, interesting.

Note: In responding to all these questions, my aim has been to educate, not condemn. The entire goal of our Amish lifestyle is to make it easier for us and our descendants to follow Jesus Christ. We believe that this culture is the best one for us. We do not claim it is the only way to attain heaven. Jesus Christ is the only way.

THE AUTHOR

LOREN BEACHY is an Old Order Amish auctioneer and elementary schoolteacher. Born in central Ohio, Beachy became a Hoosier at eight years of age when his family moved to northern Indiana. After attending Reppert Auction School at age eighteen, he attained his dream of being an auctioneer.

Beachy, a columnist for the *Goshen News*, resides with his parents and eight siblings in Goshen, Indiana, where he teaches school and conducts auctions. He is a happy member of the Old Order Amish church and enjoys fast horses, strong coffee, and hot peppers.